W9-ASM-162

THE CHANGING OPERA

BOOKS BY PAUL BEKKER

*

The Changing Opera

The Story of Music

Richard Wagner

RICHARD WAGNER

PAUL BEKKER

THE CHANGING OPERA

Translated by Arthur Mendel

W. W. NORTON & COMPANY, INC.

W. W. Norton & Company, Inc.
70 Fifth Avenue, New York

FIRST EDITION

Printed in the United States of America
For the Publishers by the Van Rees Press
NEW YORK

Contents

Illustrations

Foreword

"Nord und Süd und West zersplittern,
Throne bersten, Reiche zittern,
Flüchte du, im reinen Osten
Patriarchenluft zu kosten."
—Goethe, *West-östlicher Divan.*

"North and West and South up-breaking!
Thrones are shattering, Empires quaking;
Fly thou to the untroubled East,
There the patriarchs' air to taste."
—Translated by E. Dowden.

Ah, happy age, when the poet, at least, could speak in such terms! Today even the Orient has long since lost its enchantment. So let us keep close to the Occident and its problems. But must we have, of all things, a book on the opera? Is there nothing more pressing? One's point of view towards the world and what goes on in it, towards monetary policies, racial questions—are not these great open fields, especially in comparison with the field of opera, which by now has been thoroughly explored?

But has it been, really?

As for the timeliness of those important themes—what could be more important today than to remind ourselves of the nature of Man himself and of the achievements which, over and above all the events of the day, spring from the very nature of his being? Does not our position towards all other questions depend on our proper recognition of this one? Is not a large part of the confusion that surrounds us possible only because we approach the events of the day without clear understanding of their real nature, because we confuse creative work with mere activity, and for culture substitute propaganda? Is not the "reinen Osten" of Goethe simply the contemplation of Nature and Man as the inescapable point of departure for all thought and action?

"Untimely" books were never more timely than now. In every department of life and art we need them, for our souls are parched from feeding on the wretched present, with its hollow self-importance. They must be turned back upon themselves, not in order to spin themselves into a cocoon of romantic dreams, but in order to draw new strength from their own depths.

The present book is an attempt to point the way to the reality underlying the evolution of the opera. In connecting with the essential nature of man what seems on the surface to be the most unnatural of art-forms, in tracing the life of the opera to its sources in the life of man, and in viewing its wanderings as the creations of man's errant spirit, it affirms, over and above all purely musical considerations, the position of man himself as the origin and goal of all art, in this field as in any other. For that reason, it holds itself apart from history as such, and takes account only of such works as still live today. The pre-history of the opera is no more within its field than the series of historical connecting links. We must be able to grasp the life-element in the opera through phenomena whose continuous presence demonstrates its inner force.

Thus our concern with the inquiry into the form and inner nature of the opera is inseparably connected with that which has brought us to our present spiritual position, and with the will to maintain and improve that position against the destructive tendencies of the forces of the day. So this book addresses itself to those outside musical circles who constitute "the public"—including those who think they "know nothing about music" because they believe that music is a thing that can be approached only through study. But music is not a science, or a matter for specialists. It is the ever-alive current of action in the world of sound, and must be grasped as such. And how can it be better grasped than through the most beautiful and noblest organ of sound, belonging to all peoples, of all times—the human voice?

One thing we must all learn, from the beginning,

layman and professional without exception: to recognize this voice for what it really is, the first element in any and every musical concept. That is the given point of departure of this book. Its goal is to make the inner nature of the opera understandable as the creative mystery of the *voice taking form.*

It is on the basis of such an indissoluble bond between opera and the nature of man that the past must be understood, the present judged, and the future sensed. When once the recognition of this fact has penetrated, it may help, through the special field of opera, to focus attention upon man himself. For it will show that art is never the collective product of a group or community, no matter of what philosophical outlook, but that its existence always has been, is, and will be possible only where the existence of man as an individual human being is possible.

With the advent of the present edition some personal remarks to my American readers may be permitted.

One of those curious chances, sometimes called accidents, brought it about that on the same day when I was called as music critic to the *New Yorker Staatszeitung,* I heard that an English translation of my work on opera was soon to be published. I was all the happier for this double contact with the new world, for at the same time my books—three of which had already been published in English—were being condemned as "destructive" in my own fatherland.

The actual result has surpassed personal satisfaction. The direct contact with American musical life I have received through my activities as critic has given me a new insight into the idea of this book. It is founded upon the new recognition of the importance of the singing voice.

This idea has always obsessed me. It was already foreshadowed in the BEETHOVEN, it was first clearly expressed in KLANG UND EROS, and later in the NATURREICHE DES KLANGES.

It continues throughout the WAGNER and THE STORY OF MUSIC, until it crystallizes in the book on opera, first planned as a dramaturgy of opera. But it is not yet finished. The more one tries to fathom the secret of the human voice, the less one can discard the knowledge of the interrelation of speech and music. It becomes clear that the mode of singing and playing is determined by the variety of languages. The different climatic and physiological conditions that govern singing are those that also affect the characteristics of language. From the tower of Babel originated also the different kinds of national music. This conception of national opera and its derivation has been expressed in the present book.

Now in America I find a people with high musical talent and appreciation, and with a really ravenous appetite for music. Hitherto they have attempted with great zeal to import European music and musicians. This importation is now causing a reaction. The time has been reached when the slowly awakening cultural self-consciousness is no longer satisfied with the mere bringing over of foreign works. One no longer cares to be taken in tow by foreign cultures; one hastens to one's own creative activity.

The situation is very similar to that of German and French musical achievements in the 18th century, when Italian influence was predominant and the desire arose for a national music. Herewith arises the question of the cultural significance of such activities. It is especially apparent in relation to the opera. America is asking for its own opera. How to get it?

Surely not by imitation of foreign models. They may be good for study, but having sprung up from other soil, they are useful mainly for technical purposes. Therefore it cannot suffice for American composers to produce music with American subjects and characters, simply to show that they are able to write opera scores. American opera can be created only from creative comprehension of this country's language. That means the capacity to make this language sing, to give voice to its living soul through all its special laws of forming thought, of diction, of emotional expression—to include all this in the singing voice. Thus it has been in Germany, in France, in Russia, in all countries that have their own opera.

Therefore it is necessary to embrace the English language in its characteristic American offshoot and to make it singable. From this all laws of subject, of action, of play and of musical forms will follow as secondary matters.

Since this book deals with these problems in opera, it seems, although it does not mention American operas, to come at an appropriate time for the American reader. It once more places the singing voice in its deserved position; at the centre of opera. Thereby it directs back to the singing voice the attention of a period surfeited with instrumental music. We must realize: singing is the root of all music. But singing and speaking are twins. The acknowledgment of this fact leads to the very source of music. For music derives first and always from the musical organ of man himself, from the voice as the identical fountainhead of speech and song.

Chapter I

THE VOICE TAKING FORM

IN the beginning was the voice.

Voice is sounding breath, the audible sign of life. It mirrors the greatest difference between human beings: the sex difference. It mirrors differences in age. It mirrors individual differences among members of the same sex; in a word, it mirrors personality. It is the singing voice by which man projects himself into the sphere of sound, by which he changes his visible corporealness into invisible sound.

When man first began to fashion reality in his own image, he recognized three means of creating form as properly his own: Thought, Sound, Movement. The servant of thought was language, of sound the singing voice, of movement the body. Those are the three elementary manifestations of the *play impulse:* Man as a speaking being, man as a singing being, and man as a dancing being. They need no materials outside man.

Man as a living being is their object and their subject, matter and medium of the play impulse, which here appears as the natural life impulse itself.

The courses of the different forms of play, distinguished by their different human materials, vary from time to time. Often widely separated, they suddenly approach each other, intersect, coincide, run parallel with one another, and then quickly draw apart again. The only thing they always have in common is the urge to represent something, to act something out. In this respect, too, they are sometimes entirely taken up with the special problems of their own individual art forms; and then their mutual interrelations are more strongly felt again. Occasionally the consciousness of a common origin and goal becomes so strong that they strain towards a community of paths as well. Untouched by such changes, the media of the species always remain the same: Language, Voice, Body. Only our way of looking at them, of shaping them—whether separately or in relation with one another—changes. The historical course of these metamorphoses we call the history of the Drama, the Opera, or the Dance—that is, the history of man as a speaking, as a singing, as a dancing being.

Language is the most independent of the three elements of man's self-expression. It has no need, even when used for dramatic purposes, of Song or Dance. Its kingdom is thought. Less independent is the Dance.

It reaches out for a connection with song; at least, it wants a background of musical rhythm. Completely dependent is Song. It always needs a connection with language sounds. At the same time it seeks a connection with Dance movement, and attains its highest power of expression only in combination with both other media. Language and the Dance, then, both looked at apart from their own independent existence and only from the point of view of song, are the natural allies of the voice in the theatre. The history of the voice and its metamorphoses is the history of its changing relations to Language and to the Dance. The voice cannot get along without either of them. But it can push both into the infinitely far background. It can, on the other hand, become so dominated by both as almost to lose its own identity. It can, finally, develop organic connections with both other elements, and attempt a balancing of their various forces. The result of all this is the particular history of that species of art which has been known, since the year 1600, as the Opera. We date the beginning of the Opera from that year because it was then that the singing voice first appeared as the basic expressive component of a theatrical piece.

Upon this fact rests the historical significance of that creative art of the musical Hellenists of Florence.

What was important was not the reconstruction of Greek drama, nor, in fact, the dramatic idea in general.

For that, music would not have been necessary, nor even a circle of music-lovers as its creators. What was important was Song. It arose out of a primarily musical reaction, namely, out of a desire for simplification, for the displacing of the constructed by the spontaneous. "The one thing everyone agreed on was that, since the music of the day was quite inadequate to the expression of the words, and in its development actually repugnant to the thought, means must be found, in the attempt to bring music back closer to that of classical times, to bring out the chief melody prominently so that the poetry should be clearly understandable." Thus the Florentine Doni described the new stage-music of 1640. The voice was to lead, in contrast to its place in the complexity of contrapuntal forms, as an individual, melodic manifestation. For this purpose it needed language. In order for an illustrative form to grow out of Song and Language, the only thing lacking was expression in dramatically constructed form.

And thus it was through the word that the voice took shape, the word in natural simplicity, intelligibly arranged in sentences, uttered by a single voice clearly and understandably, in dialogue form, explained even to the extent of having physical illustrations of its meaning. Therein lay the approach to the idea of the Classic drama. It was, already in the beginnings of

Opera, only a means—not towards the ends of music, however, but towards those of song.

But how is it possible to draw a line of demarcation between song and music? Is not song always music?

Certainly. But music is not always song. The tension between the two arises from the varying climatic conditions in various countries, and from the consequently varying physiological conditions for music-making. In all Mediterranean cultures, song dominates. The development of instrumental abilities is not hindered by this fact, but they are always closely connected to song, and are conceived in close relation to it. Song determines the nature and the fundamental concepts of the music. The longing for the revival of one-voiced song leads in Italy to the birth of the harmonic sense, and therewith to the creation of the opera.

Migration to the north causes a shift in the relationship. Language, climate, and natural endowment are less favorable to the voice. It loses its leading position. Beside the conception of music as song, another conception grows up out of the world of instrumental tone. Continuously nourished on the increasing complexity of the instrumental side of music, this conception gains such predominance that the voice itself becomes simply a part of the total apparatus, one instrument among many. Assigned to a place in the mechanically organized total, it loses its original shaping force, and must bow to instrumental mechanization. So, here in the north, the opera itself becomes just so much music, like a symphony, or a piano sonata. It differs from those forms of composition simply in the greater performing forces it requires, and in the fact that it is produced with scenery.

Parallel with this mutation of song into music goes a change in the significance of the visual means of the opera. The use of the singing voice postulates the unreality of the being represented by it. To represent that being in song is to lift him entirely out of the world of actuality, and stamp him as belonging definitely to the world of appearance. He can no more leave that world than a figure thrown on a screen can take on corporeality. The being who sings while he moves, sings while he acts, sings while he speaks, is irretrievably removed from actuality. He remains tied to the dream-world of the imagination which produced him. So everything he does—his manner, the nature of his movement, dress, environment—must accord with this purely illusory nature of his; for all this exists only to make his illusory existence possible, and to give it atmosphere. Herder, a good critic of opera, says: "Once a world is established in which everything sings, and everything dances, the surroundings too must take on this character: they must cast a magic spell."

Accordingly, dramatic possibilities, to the same

degree as in the spoken drama, do not exist in the world of the singing voice. It is only the illusion of drama that is possible, in the same sense in which a singing being counts only as the illusion of a real being. This does not mean that the possibility of dramatic effect in a work using singing voices is removed; but it is on a different level, and can never enter into competition with the spoken drama. The same is true of the external means of illustration, from the costume and the stage-setting to the bodily movements of the singers. Everything is governed by the underlying law of conscious illusion, the law of the sound-world in which alone opera can live and breathe.

This illusory character was preserved as long as the close relationship with the fundamental nature of the opera remained. It was lost in the same proportion that the closeness of that relationship was relaxed: as for example when, through the migration of the art-form into northern lands, the primacy of song was sacrificed in favor of instrumental music. Out of the sound world of the orchestra arose ideas of the drama and all its illustrative elements: the idea of acting, of staging, of representation. But is all that necessarily mistaken? Is such an approximation of the opera to the drama, based on reasoning and language, whether on speculative or physiological grounds, not possible, not practical, not conceivable perhaps even as a step forward?

If the aims of the opera and the drama were identical, achieved in the same ways, by the same means, there would be a duplication of expressive forces such as exists nowhere else in the Economy of Art; and it is therefore difficult to assume here, for it would be purposeless. In those places in art where similarities exist—as for example in sculpture, which works in different kinds of stone, and in wood as well—it can be seen that these very differences reach down into the kernels of the art-forms, and accordingly lead to genuinely differing results. The family relationships are only of an external nature and hardly really exist at all, when the works are truly considered as works of art. This must hold correspondingly true of the opera and the spoken drama. If, on the other hand, both tend towards the same goal, work towards it with the same means, and run parallel to each other right to the end, then one must necessarily be better and one worse. The worse, then, as the weaker, would be superfluous. This was the opinion (altogether justifiable) of the most zealous partisan of the dogma of the dramatic mission of the opera—Richard Wagner. If the opera really were that fulfilment of the drama which he considered it, if it really were a union of Shakespeare and Beethoven, its superiority to the spoken drama would be demonstrated. The latter, which Wagner called "literature," would then be just superfluous as was, in Wagner's opinion, pure instrumental music.

Wagner's conclusion is perfectly correct as soon as one accepts his premise. The latter maintains that opera based on song is an aberration and can become dramatic action only with the aid of language. But does this premise really hold?

The era since Wagner has decided against it, and the output of composers has confirmed this rejection. Thus the questions remain: What about the opera, really? Is it only a sort of half-developed drama, shunted off onto a wrong path? Or not even that? Is it a paradox which is really not to be taken seriously, but to be observed as a delusion, remarkable only because so many men of genius have concerned themselves with it? Or is the opera simply a social relic of bygone times, maintained merely out of thoughtless habit?

Against the latter idea is the fact that opera was never cultivated exclusively at courts. It always existed in the form of folk-opera. Against that idea, above all, is the fact that the opera already at the turn of the eighteenth century had become organized as an art-form for the middle class. Against the paradox-theory we have an output of almost 400 years, of which the output of more than 150 years still lives. It would be an instance unique in the history of the human mind, if the greatest geniuses of several centuries had continually attempted, many successfully, an art-form whose sole attraction consisted in the irreconcilability of its contradictions, in the impossibility of solving its problem.

If the opera is neither the fulfilment, nor a sister of equal birth, nor even an inferior half-sister, of the drama—then what is it? The answer to this question would have to establish whether the opera has within itself an element that distinguishes it from all other art-forms. That element would have to be both material and spiritual—and of such shaping force that it could not only found an art-form, but also propagate it, and develop it into an organism artistically complete in itself. That element would have to be common to—indeed the distinguishing feature of—all operas that have ever been, no matter what other artistic aims they pursued, whether they aimed at being dramas or *singspiele,* whether they were dedicated to tragedy or comedy, whether they dated from 1600 or from 1900, and no matter to which nation they belonged.

Such an element exists. It makes itself known through the fact that all these operas are sung, that is, that they all rest on the presence and the possibilities of the human voice. This characteristic is at the same time the only one which is common to all operas, of all times. For the rest, they show beyond differences of period the greatest variety of aesthetic aims, as well as of practical realization, musically, dramatically, and scenically. The voice alone is the tie that binds them all together. More:

if one takes this voice away from the opera, it ceases to be opera. It is robbed of its essential characteristic. And this, too, is true of all works. Still more: the changes in the treatment of the voice show clearly recognizable historical groupings. They show a continuously changing creative approach to the voice. They show—as is clear from critical consideration—beyond all differences an absolutely unified fundamental direction, throughout their changing vocal characterization.

Consequently, the singing voice is the root from which the opera has sprouted and grown. It is the force that carries the opera forward. It is the power that ever anew leads it to completion, according to the mode in which the nature of the voice is perceived. The form of the opera arises from the voice: it becomes physically perceptible in such shape as is dictated by the development of the voice.

Thus, the opera is the realization of the potentialities of the singing voice, whose laws it brings to fulfilment, whose possibilities it brings to concrete realization, whose susceptibility to change at the hands of an ever-changing creative fancy it represents. All other similarities to other art-forms are coincidences, which have nothing to do with the essence and secret of this one.

Whether the opera composer has always been clearly conscious of the significance of the voice as the determining element of the form is irrelevant. In many cases he has not been. During the course of the nineteenth century, especially, this basic understanding gradually fell into oblivion, especially in Germany. Only today is it slowly beginning to be grasped again. But the fact was effective and fruitful even where it was not consciously recognized—otherwise no operatic achievement would have been possible. It is clear, even, that the reflection of other forces and other goals actually produced many important rediscoveries and creative developments, so far as the voice is concerned. The underlying law of the species is mightier than the professed aesthetic theory of the day, which, through its reflections of a new mode of thought, serves to bring about the next step in the development of the voice.

Around this fixed axis are grouped the purely temporal characteristics: the dramatic, the musical, the decorative, the material, the social—everything, that is, that characterizes the sociological manifestation that is opera, and the changes in its form. Untouched by these things remains the singing human voice, remains the recognition of opera as the constant process by which the voice takes form amid the ever-changing play of external factors. Thus the history of opera becomes the history of the Voice and its manifold relations to other elements.

Beneath all these things, the singing voice is, with Language and the Dance, the direct expression of man himself. In its tones he utters the clear revelation of his spirit, in the metamorphoses of its forms he mirrors the metamorphoses of that spirit through all the ages in which the singing voice is heard and achieves visible form.

Chapter II

GLUCK

THE dramaturgical history of modern serious opera begins with the second part of the work of Christoph Willibald Gluck. All the earlier operas are simply musical material, and we may leave them to learned chronicling. This old opera is based upon an art of singing that has become strange to us of the present. It requires voices that no longer exist, namely, the voices of the *castrati*.

The *castrato* voice, to judge from the music written for it, as well as from contemporary reports, must have been a wonderful sound-phenomenon. It is understandable that a time that had such voices at its disposal felt only slight need of instrumental music. For the *castrato* voice was itself an instrumentalized human voice. The fundamental characteristic of the voice—its sex character—had been taken away from it. In return it received the agility of an instrument—an instrument, which, however, was not a dead mechanism, but remained a living organism. The remarkable, almost unreal effect of this voice rested not alone on the contradiction of nature, hardly conceivable today, which permitted a Hercules to sing florid soprano arias. The basic element was the de-personalizing of the voice. This it was that brought about the conscious surrender of the possibility of making the singing voice identical with, or even similar to, the natural voice of the character represented.

It will not do to look down on this attitude with any false sense of superiority. Interest in the singing voice had reached such a pitch of fanaticism that the dramatic action, and the fate of the character represented, were only external means of connecting things. They had no further importance. Naturalism was completely absent from the dramatic point of view of the time. The only important thing was that the singing should be as beautiful as could be conceived.

This requirement was met by the *castrato* voice better than by any other. Its tonal range included the most favorable registers; it united within itself the brilliance and soft texture of the woman's voice with the strength of the man's; unlimited capacities for expressive shading with equally unlimited virtuosity. Compared with its best examples, the most beautiful voices of today would necessarily sound clumsy and ordinary—at least so far as it would be possible to overlook the unnatural character of the *castrato* voice. For a proper understanding of the culture of that period, it is necessary, however, to grasp as an artistic phenomenon the rare product, raised by mutilation to a sort of super-human perfection, that was the *castrato* voice. Even to the reconstructing imagination, to be sure, this is only imperfectly possible. For the very thing in which the spell of the voice consists today—its erotic charm—was in those days considered a disturbing limitation upon vocal achievement.

Opera before Gluck, and the first half of Gluck's work, was not entirely for *castrati*. But it was decisively influenced by that type of voice, in which it found its fulfilment. That voice determined the nature of the material, of the action, of the scenic conception. The principles of artistic entertainment coincided with the purposes of courtly merriment. Parallel with the extremely one-sided development of this court type of opera, there arose its realistic counterpart: the humorous *Intermezzo*. But it remained always a subordinate manifestation, and could not disturb the supremacy of the *castrato* opera. It maintained its basic character even while it reflected various local colors: Venetian, Neapolitan, Roman with its branches in Madrid and London, and, in coarse, popular adaptations, those of Hamburg, Leipsic, Nuremburg, Brunswick. It remained everywhere the opera of the anti-natural, instrumentalized singing voice: the unreality of opera carried to its final conclusion.

The domain of the *castrato* extends even into Gluck's works. The title rôle of his ORPHEUS, the oldest serious opera still alive on present-day stages, was written for a *castrato*. A last representative of this vanished world is to be found in the opera of Mozart's youth, IDOMENEO, which, just because of its connection with the earlier opera, is lost to our stage. The gates to these works have closed forever, and no exorcism will open them again. Not because their dramatic nature, their musical form, or any other feature has aged, but because the sound of the voice that made them live and determined their nature has forever disappeared. For that reason it is an idle pursuit to try to reconstruct them for the sake of their musical worth, whether they are by Monteverdi, or Hasse, or Handel. Their breath is exhausted. Only the ruins of them remain, without inner connection.

It is in and through Gluck that the transition takes place.

Its distinctive feature is not the change from the aria-opera to the dramatically conceived organism, not the change from the independence of the singer to the dominant authority of the musical creator, nor yet the simplification of coloratura elaboration into a clear line. All these changes took place, but they were results, not causes. The transition was really from the unnatural to the natural—from vocal virtuosi to singing human beings. The author of this change was Rousseau.

In his musical aesthetics, Rousseau followed other paths. But he determined the direction of music as the apostle of the evangel of the Return to Nature, disseminated in France by Diderot and the Encyclopaedists, in Germany by Lessing and Herder.

This Return to Nature shows a similarity to that other Return that had given birth, a century and a half earlier, to the opera. Then the determining factor had been the feeling of a need for a leading melody, producing a new naturalness as compared with the effect of polyphony. Now, in contrast to the domination of the voice, become an end in itself, the demand for a new recognition of man as a human being announced itself. Into the shadow-world of vocal spectres came the first sounds of the approaching cultural upheaval.

When Gluck became aware of it, he had already completed a considerable part of his work. His achievement consists in the fact that he thrust the doors open and allowed the daylight of human naturalness to fall upon the opera world of his time. In that light it was natural that many things should assume an aspect different from that which they had had under the half-light of the eunuch atmosphere that had hitherto obtained. Artificially curlicued lines straightened out. Artistic virtuosity for its own sake gave way to a newly crystallizing purity of song. Reason and logic asserted their rights as men began to sing with their natural voices. Intellect and the feeling of a clear and purified attitude towards art arose to form a critical conscience, which tested the art-work for its possibilities in the light of the demands of a new ideal of form.

"The course of the century leads us to a man who, scorning the rubbish of wordless tones, saw the necessity of an inner bond between, on the one hand, purely human emotion and the story itself and, on the other, the tones he worked with." The art-work of Gluck, thus described by Herder, was nothing new. It was the old Florentine opera. Enriched through the experiments and experiences of the intervening time, purged of the aberrations to which the autocracy of the denatured voice had necessarily led, it had now arrived, having been led back to nature and man, at the fulfilment of its original purpose. But no more than that. It was still court opera, the Olympic festival of gods and heroes, for the entertainment of princes.

The decorative element acts as a sort of magically glamorous frame. The subjects are always of mythological or allegorical character, and almost without exception taken from Classical antiquity. The ballet remains an organic part as the fairy-like element, the choruses lend a Greek character to the style, just as they do in French tragedy. The type of aria melody corresponds, in its diatonic simplicity and symmetry, to the most beautiful models of Italian song, as practiced right up to Handel and Hasse. The harmony, based on the purely schematic significance of the bass, rests upon the basic feeling of a transparent clarity in the voice-leading. The recitative, grown into a great and intensely powerful medium of expression, receives special stimulation from the rhetorical declamation of French opera. The streams of the two representative art-forms—the Italian *opera seria* and the lyric tragedy of Lully and Rameau—flow together.

This unification of naturalistic song, dance based on pantomime, and rationally ordered action is the product of Gluck's combative and despotic genius. But there is no sign of a desire for revolutionary changes in the operatic organism, which is simply purified, deflated, tightened by the strong and critically cleansing attitude of a man who reacts rationalistically to things.

Thus Gluck brings to a close the history of the old opera, being the first to reveal the truthfulness of its nature and bring it within humanly moving reach. Of his operas, five are to be regarded as of lasting vitality: ORPHEUS, ALCESTE, ARMIDE, IPHIGÉNIE EN AULIDE, and IPHIGÉNIE EN TAURIDE. ORPHEUS still bears the mark of the *castrato* opera in the treatment of the title rôle. All the others are, as even the titles show, chiefly con-

Gluck

cerned with women. Alceste, Armide, and Clytemnestra —the leading figure in IPHIGÉNIE EN AULIDE—all are of the highly dramatic type. In IPHIGÉNIE EN AULIDE the Iphigénie is a lyric soprano; in IPHIGÉNIE EN TAURIDE she is a mature but youthful dramatic soprano representing womanhood not yet completely developed. Coloratura singing has disappeared, save only in slight ornamentation in the subordinate parts; aria melody and the declamatory, plastically significant recitative reign alone.

The men's voices remain for the most part episodic. There are only three fully developed men's rôles in Gluck: Admetus in ALCESTE; Agamemnon in IPHIGÉNIE EN AULIDE; Orestes in IPHIGÉNIE EN TAURIDE. Admetus, although overshadowed within the work by the towering greatness of Alceste, becomes in the Orcus recitatives, and still more in his outburst of grief, the first dramatic tenor on the grand scale. His voice, in its tragic accents, attains to a gripping naturalness of expression, reveals a last tonal secret of the vocal organ. Mozart took this character of Gluck's as the model for his Idomeneo.

Even more striking than Admetus is the figure of Orestes in IPHIGÉNIE EN TAURIDE. Beside the Agamemnon of IPHIGÉNIE EN AULIDE, Orestes stands as the first great baritone figure of tragic opera. This placing in a leading position of the semi-dark male voice anticipates the romantic naturalism followed by Mozart in Don Giovanni. How deep a relationship is conceived between the color and quality of this, the most masculine male voice, and the character it represents, is shown by the development of this first great problem figure into the central feature of the Eumenides scene in the second act.

Gluck's material world and world of illusion correspond to the desire for naturalism. They rest upon a simple contrasting of opposites: in Nature, of day and night; in the action, of life and death; in the staging, of mechanics to provide for sinking through the floor and for the effect of flying. Orpheus loses and then wins Euridice; Alceste gives herself to death for her husband's sake; Armide's magic realm of love is destroyed; Iphigénie is sacrificed to the Gods; Orestes contends with the demons of the underworld. These are all actions of primitive simplicity, without the element of sexual love. Even the love-world of Armide is simply a given background. It is Fate that develops contrasts out of the nature of things. Contributory actions on the part of human beings, such as intrigues or psychologically conditioned actions, are absent. The action is not looked at from the point of view of the individual, or determined by necessities of character. These are emotional types, clothed in the symbols of mythology. The means of this symbolization consist in the color and treatment of the voices. For this purpose a simple, harmonized melodic line suffices, and the music confines itself to simple dynamic contrasts. It is homophonic, no matter whether the individual solo voice or the entire chorus sings. For this purpose, finally, it culminates in two means of expression: the predominating female voice, and the singing chorus.

The chorus is the organ of harmony, always treated in planes, no matter whether it is hurling the "No!" of the underworld back to Orpheus, or painting Elysium in floating sequences, or mourning the death of Alceste, or whipping up the mad dreams of Orestes. Tonal effects of this sort were never again produced after Gluck. The conception of the chorus as a harmonic entity is split up. From this point on, instead, it turns into the vital contrast of men's and women's voices. In Gluck's works there is no interest in this warm, living sphere of sound. For the same reason variety is not important to him. He writes no great concerted pieces; the orchestra remains always an accompanying unit, giving purely dynamic support, occasionally coming to the fore with chamber-music soli in the woodwinds, corresponding to the singing voice. The bearer of the rhythmically moving harmony remains chiefly the chorus.

Its counterpart as the true fulfilment of the art-conception of Gluck is the dramatic female voice. It is the female voice that leads, and in it there is embodied the creative urge of the work and of its author. In this dramatically active female voice, always partaking of the emotion of the situation, yet still not open to passion, there comes to fruition that fertile kernel which was implicit even in the unnatural *castrato* voice: the desire for emotional expression through the singing voice, above or apart from its sexual nature—the desire for the virginity of the voice. But now it is taken out of the sphere of that degeneracy, that artistic twilight, and deposited in the subsoil of the great reality of human nature as it is. Thus it is clothed in a heroic, humanly active, and yet mythical figure—for even Armide's love remains beyond earthly reality.

And thus that voice becomes the symbol of a world of feeling whose pure beauty testifies to a unique creative vision. To Orpheus, a transitional figure, this perhaps does not apply. But for Alceste, Armide, Clytemnestra, Iphigénie of IPHIGÉNIE EN AULIDE, and Iphigénie of IPHIGÉNIE EN TAURIDE, who outshines them all—for these female figures of the lyric stage, just as for Gluck's choruses, there is no yardstick by which one can compare them with anything that preceded or followed them. They cannot be compared with anything earlier, for it was just this transition to the female voice as the leading factor that reconciled the art-idea of the old opera with the requirements of humanly appealing drama; nor with anything later, for this indeterminate state, hovering between human and individual expression through the voice, this existence in the sphere of pure feeling, could be achieved once, at the end of a long line of development—but it could not be maintained. The voice and the human being had now found each other. Now they must continue their journey together. This journey inevitably led further and further into the domain of human personality, with all its earthly limitations.

It has been the practice to represent Gluck as the founder of music-drama, as the opponent of the old opera, as the reformer who put an end to the supremacy of the singer, perhaps even as the forerunner of Wagner. To be sure, there is some basis for each of these opinions. Gluck's own utterances, some of them very argumentative, offer convenient handles to which to attach such interpretations. But as a matter of fact, what happens—seldom enough, indeed—is that the more the dramatic qualities of Gluck's works are stressed, the less successful is the attempt to make them at home on the contemporary stage. So that either Gluck as a forerunner of music-drama has been eclipsed by those who came after him, or else that view of Gluck is incorrect, and therefore the manner in which the attempt is made to bring him close to the opera-goer of today is mistaken.

There is, of course, no way of making Gluck a popular composer, and assuring his works of mass popularity.

That they have never enjoyed. They were written not for the public, but for the court and for the aristocracy. They are the last and only living examples of that form of art. Therefore they are recognizable only in productions which preserve the fundamental character of the old court opera—which grew out of Baroque—in the stage setting, in the acting, and in the treatment of the chorus as well as of the decorative element. These are stylistic prerequisites; unless they are observed, the works lose their meaning.

Out of this soil, then, must grow the performances of the central singing characters. They must and will always produce their effect if their human element is made recognizable and believable by the character of the singing and of the voices through which they are projected. The way will not be shown by theorizing. It is to be found only through recognition of the melodic line as the key to the dramatist's secret, and through continuous and searching scrutiny of the scenic illusion in its relation to the fundamental creative purpose: the search for nature.

Chapter III

MOZART

I

WITH Gluck there comes to an end the history of courtly opera—opera as the reflection of the world viewed through the eyes of the aristocracy.

In that world there were high and noble feelings such as befit men who live in fine palaces with great gardens—men whose way of living presupposes the absence of the elementary wants. Gluck was still able to base his creative activity upon such a separation from reality, and thus bring to fulfilment the original tendency of the opera as the art-form of complete unreality.

The moment this ideal was realized, it was also destroyed. The urge towards nature, of which Gluck's opera bore the imprint, continued to act as a disintegrating force. It raised moderate agitation to the pitch of passionate emotion, and transformed idealized types into individual personalities. It held the items of mythical allegory up to comparison with reality. The civilization of Western Europe, experiencing an inner unrest due to new problems arising from the organization of society, was reaching the stage of critical thinking. In the face of these problems, the lovely magic of these court works of art could hardly maintain its position, for their world was beyond life, and it had no answers for the questions now presented. This was the end of the *fata morgana* of a classical antiquity such as had never existed. Its place was taken by the opera of the Age of Enlightenment, the opera of critical realism, the opera of the free man, with the humanistic ideal of citizenship in the world. That opera was created and brought to fulfilment by Wolfgang Amadeus Mozart.

Outside of the youthful work König Thamos, Mozart wrote only one opera in which he paid homage to Gluck: Idomeneo. It was clear that he could not continue in this direction. The tragic Cothurnus is not really suited to Mozart, beautiful as is the music he makes. Immediately following Idomeneo, Mozart wrote Die Entführung aus dem Serail. With that work he had achieved his real footing, which he never afterwards lost: rejection of the pathetic style, acknowledgment of realism, of the things that belonged not to lofty feelings far removed from earthly reality, but to life, to actuality; not to singing ideas but to singing personalities.

In connection with this realism arose the question of language. Until then, Italian had been the language of opera. It was very singable, and, besides, opera composers received their training in Italy. The state of the German language at the time was hardly favorable to its being shaped to musical uses, nor to its being used at court. But among the people a simple form of musical entertainment had grown up. It was a mixture of spoken dialogue interspersed with songs and little concerted pieces. The performers were actors who could also sing, and the whole was called *Singspiel* (song-play). In content usually of a coarse and sturdy humor, it was a phenomenon corresponding to those *intermezzi* that had developed in Italy as entr'actes in the *opera seria,* and that were leading gradually to the popular *opera buffa.* In 1733, Pergolesi, in the SERVA PADRONA, had created the classic model of this species. On German soil, Hiller of Leipsic, about 1750, and Keiser of Hamburg were particularly successful. In 1760, Rousseau followed in France with his DEVIN DU VILLAGE. To this series, finally, belongs the parodistic BEGGAR'S OPERA in England.

Common to all the works of this lighter species is the emphasis of the sturdy, robust folk-element, the rejection of art-singing and the stress laid upon the dramatic stage action. Corresponding to this is the dominance of the sense of the words in the musical numbers as well. Taken all together, then, the *Singspiel* represented a conscious opposition to opera and its strangeness of language. The desire for a musical stage for the middle class, and the urge towards a simple naturalism, were decisive. They demanded above all that the characters on the stage should use the language of the land, so that every listener could understand what they were singing and talking about.

But this raised a far-reaching problem.

Insofar as it involved simply substituting the native language for a foreign one, the whole proceeding could be considered as representing simply a reasonable self-consciousness. But with the change of language there was bound up the question of the singableness of German words. The whole style of singing hitherto had presupposed the grammatical and phonetic structure of the Italian language. But now this basis disappeared. It remained to be discovered whether the German language was capable of supporting any style of vocal music more elaborate than the simple song which was all that it had hitherto supported. There were many qualities of Italian operatic song that could not in any way be taken over into German. The renouncing of these things necessarily had a profound effect upon the whole vocal style, and thus upon the entire shape, of the work itself. Did other possibilities of vocal technique, of vocal expression, hitherto unknown, exist to take the place of those renounced? That is the basic question. Put in concrete form, it reads: how is the singing voice connected with the elements of the vernacular? All theories about opera and drama, form and content, are simply attempts to disguise this basic question, by referring to other apparently more far-reaching, ideas.

Mozart's answer to the question reads: ENTFÜHRUNG, FIGARO, DON GIOVANNI, COSÌ FAN TUTTE, ZAUBERFLÖTE. He wrote two great German operas and three great Italian operas that still live on the stage. As a matter of fact, FIGARO, DON GIOVANNI, and COSÌ FAN TUTTE must really be regarded as German operas. It would never occur to an Italian to consider these works Italian. Mozart wrote them to Italian texts only because what he wanted said and sung could not be said and sung in German.

That was the solution arrived at by the rationalistic Freemason, the enlightened citizen of the world, the humanistic worshipper of nature, beauty, and wisdom, who in spite of his enlightenment was a deeply religious man, and in spite of his world-citizenship a passionate German. The thing that marks him off as a German musician has nothing to do with whether he composed to German or Italian text.

He took whatever text seemed to him necessary and suitable for each individual case. It was the music to which it was set that determined the nationality. Gluck's

or Handel's music to their works in foreign languages cannot be described as Italian, or English, or French; but it cannot be described as German either. It is a world language, just as Latin once was the general language of culture. Mozart, on the other hand, is a German musician even when he sings his song to Italian text. He chooses the Italian text for reasons of artistic suitability to his ends—because in particular cases it sounds better, or even because he could sing it in no other tongue.

This true universality of his nature permitted him to gather inspiration for his singing characters from everywhere. Mozart's singing figures are not (as, later, Wagner's were) simply variations of the same basic type. They are in each of the five chief works almost completely new. In them he shows a power of invention such as never reappeared in opera. It was possible only at that instant when the newly awakening desire for vocal characterization came into contact with an art of singing whose possibilities were not yet exhausted.

In fact the whole phenomenon called Mozart is conceivable only as the result of a never-to-be-repeated state of equilibrium existing among all the forces governing the opera: perfection of the art of song, which had lost its position of dominance through Gluck; awakening of a desire for naturalistic acting, which, however, did not yet demand any one-sided exaggeration; increased significance of the orchestra, which nevertheless remained subordinate to the singing action on the stage; availability, according to individual requirements, of both German and Italian texts, of the *Singspiel* or Opera type, of the simple room-scene or the resources of the mechanized stage. The ever less limited choice of subject made possible wide freedom of action. Add to this an audience in which there was a strong impulse towards intellectuality, a public just released from the bondage of the limitations of lower-class taste. It was necessary for all these things to come together in a remarkable adjustment of forces in order to make the appearance of Mozart possible.

It is not taking anything away from Mozart's genius to call attention to this uniquely favorable tendency of all the attendant circumstances towards a harmonious synthesis. The same circumstances made success in such a competition all the harder. This was the time when Lessing, Wieland, Herder, were just becoming known, when Schiller and Goethe were taking the stage by storm, when Gluck and Italian opera still held sway, and when the world outside the theatre was filled with new, revolutionary ideas. In a time of such high intellectual tension, only that musician could succeed on the operatic stage who had genius enough to give to the opera that which distinguished it from other art-forms: song. But song, in turn, must make its appearance as the essential content of that which had become the goal of life and thought in all fields: Personality.

2

All the vocal characters of Mozart are personalities: personalities through the shape given to their voice parts, the registers in which these parts are written, the sort of vocal technique with which they are treated, the mode of expression given to them. The power of representation purely through the color and direction of the voice presupposes that every turn of the vocal line is thought of and created in direct relation to the unfolding of the character. Mozart finds stimuli for such vocal characterization in all the vocal types existing hitherto; only the French opera bearing Gluck's stamp remains comparatively unused, after the unfavorable experience with IDOMENEO. On the other hand, Mozart is more unprejudiced than Gluck where virtuosity is concerned. The coloratura soprano in particular seems to him usable to heighten dramatic expression. It may be that this insight came to him as a result of practical experience with appropriately gifted singers.

Thus the part of Konstanze in the ENTFÜHRUNG was created as a dramatic coloratura soprano part for Mozart's sister-in-law, Aloysia Lange. To be sure, one succeeds rarely enough nowadays in finding a singer with the requisite combination of power in the middle register and lightness in the higher. The opinion has been expressed that Mozart, out of a desire to be agreeable, went too far to meet the wishes of a singer. But any simplification of this part would have diminished considerably the significance of the figure of Konstanze, and thus taken away from the weight of the work as a whole. Virtuosity, here as in the case of the Queen of the Night, serves as a musico-dramatic means for accenting a figure not very favorably conceived from the scenic viewpoint.

The case of Donna Anna is different. Here the coloratura part is inserted consciously as a heightening of the expression in the dramatic sense, just as, on the other hand, Fiordiligi in Così FAN TUTTE serves as a means of lightening the atmosphere.

The four figures show four different individualizations of the same basic type. Each of them is a musical character complete in itself. Through its singing significance, each maintains its place in the front rank even where, as in the case of the Queen of the Night, its actual appearances on the stage are episodic. This vocal type, the dramatic singer with coloratura abilities, bound up with the time before Mozart and exemplified as late as Bellini's NORMA, is today becoming extinct. Thus the rôles of Konstanze and the Queen of the Night are nowadays sung, because of the problems of agility involved, by coloratura sopranos, who lack the necessary intensity in the middle register; and Donna Anna is sung by dramatic sopranos, who lack assurance in the coloratura passages. This is an example of the gradual destruction of a vocal type, and with it of the sensuous impression created by it, through the different direction taken by the practice of subsequent times.

These vocal creations of dramatic pathos have their roots in tradition. They have thus a somewhat centaur-like existence, and in performance it is hard to arrive at a harmonious combination of vocal and dramatic representation. Mozart's most personal creation, on the other hand, was the young woman's voice, into the tonal purity of which the emotion of love introduces the first stirrings of longing, grief, passion, even jealous anger. The beginnings of this feminine series of Mozart's are already contained in the elegiac lyricism of portions of the rôle of Konstanze. But the series really begins with the Countess in FIGARO, and continues with Elvira and Dorabella, culminating in the tender Pamina—the truly ideal figure of the operatic stage.

In the fabulous clarity of the tonal character of Pamina, in her sudden awakening out of the unrippled calm of childhood into mature depth of feeling and a spirit of self-sacrifice, she stands out, even among the creations of Mozart, as miraculous. Only the possibilities that lie in the youthful female voice as material for artistic expression explain her. The Countess in

FIGARO does not, it is true, run such a wide emotional gamut. But she reveals marked versatility, from lyric elegy, through light conversation in dialogue scenes, to soaring ecstasy. As a vocal personality she, too, is a unique and incomparable being. Like Pamina, she displays the fascination of the female voice in line and motion, arising not from the glitter of technical virtuosity, but from the thoughts of love and longing associated with woman's personality.

Fundamentally the same is true of Elvira, that stepchild among Mozart's women in love. The dramatic temperament of Donna Anna is too forceful for Elvira not to seem slight and episodic in comparison, set off against one another as they are. Dorabella, on the other hand, is, like Fiordiligi, definitely influenced by the whole atmosphere of dalliance in COSÌ FAN TUTTE, so that she, like all the other characters in this work except Alfonso, is but a mask of the Mozartean woman-type.

This central group of Mozart's female voice-types is completed by lighter voices, who cover the field of lyric expression even to the coloratura sauciness of the soubrette. But there is no basic type for these characters: they are assorted and individual personalities. Lightest of them all, and thus most nimble in coloratura technique and highest in vocal range, are Blondchen and Despina. Related to them, though of course only an episodic figure, is the dancing Papagena. Between these two groups stand Susanna, Cherubino, and Zerlina. According to the usual classification, they are soubrettes, too; but they are hardly coloratura rôles, nor are they called upon for any particularly high notes. They thus represent temperamental variations of the lyric female voice, drenched in the same sound-color of love and longing, but here inclining to graceful mirth instead of elegiac melancholy. In Zerlina that color receives a certain slight admixture of hidden desire, in Cherubino of vague unrest. In Susanna, the most richly endowed of the three, all the charms of feminine impishness come to life, and they give her a lyric importance which takes its place beside that of the Countess.

These are, apart from the purely episodic Marzelline, Mozart's feminine singing characters. To them are to be added the three women and the three boys in the ZAUBERFLÖTE. The women sum up the agility and the variety of the female voice. The boys represent the sexless purity of three-part harmonies in the upper vocal reaches. It is a striking fact that Mozart, except in these two ensemble groups, never used the alto voice. It is striking, too, that although one recognizes fundamental similarities, nevertheless each character has a vocal personality different from every other. It is striking, finally, to notice what it was that Mozart wished to obtain from every species of female voice: the expression of love in all its nuances.

The conception of love as a heroic emotion was furthest from Mozart's mind, doubtless because that conception is furthest from reality as well. The nearer he came to feminine tenderness and delicacy—that is, the more closely his own fantasy approached human credibility—the greater became the richness and variety with which his female characters sang. From this point on, their exaltation of expression, remaining always within natural human bounds, were just as new as their mischief and gayety. Yet the voice of woman awaking to painful or happy consciousness of love became for Mozart, and through Mozart, the essential female voice as such.

Herein lies one of the basic secrets of Mozart's artistic achievements. The magic of the arias of Pamina, the Countess, or Susanna, does not consist simply of the beauty of their melodic outline, or of other qualities definable in musical terms. It is based upon the fact that in them it is woman's voice itself that sings, and upon the intuition with which the emotions of woman are translated into tone.

Characteristics quite different, and on the surface more varied, are shown by Mozart's male voices. Noteworthy is the rare use of the tenor voice. It never occurs to Mozart to use the tenor voice except for youths, and even for these chiefly in the German *Singspiele,* DIE ENTFÜHRUNG and DIE ZAUBERFLÖTE. For Mozart, the tenor is a purely lyric voice, suitable to the performance of simple, song-like music, but not appropriate for dramatic or heroic passages. Mozart always treats the tenor as a light voice. Belmonte, Oktavio (from the dramatic point of view abortive), Fernando, and Tamino, are youthful singers of fine songs, and youngsters in love—not men. In the spoken scene, Tamino, induced by his partner, moves for the moment in the direction of dramatic emphasis. But thereafter his importance diminishes exactly in proportion as the action pushes forward, in contrast to the figure of Pamina which takes on continually increasing significance.

The tenor characters, especially Belmonte and Tamino, were without a doubt created by Mozart with great love and sympathy. They carry within them the poetry of youth, which needs no foundation. Thus their sphere of action is circumscribed. Mozart did not entrust to the tenor any real dramatic force—at least, not as a solo voice. Apart from purely lyric functions associated with light, clear color, and mercurial agility, he uses it as a *buffo,* in DIE ENTFÜHRUNG (Pedrillo) and DIE ZAUBERFLÖTE (Monostatos), according to the custom of the *Singspiel,* and again, by changing its timbre into a poisonous sharpness, in FIGARO (Basilio). With these, Mozart's demand for tenors is covered. Their function is to sing well, to be good-looking, and in addition—and this is their main task—to support and lead the ensemble.

Mozart's real vocal conception of a man is in terms of the bass voice. He makes as yet no distinction between baritone and bass, at least as far as denomination goes. He groups all the darker male voices in one category. Notice that in the vocal characterization of men, too, their relation to love is fundamental, and the classification of the voices, from lowest to highest, is according to this relation. Lowest of all is the cast-off old lover, the grumbling devil Osmin, with his virtuoso agility and unusually low range—a part written for a singer of a special vocal quality. Of Osmin one may say what Beethoven said of Weber's Kaspar, but with greater justification: that he stands there like a house, and contains all the subsequent unholy basses of the German stage, from Kaspar to Alberich, within himself. Senility is captured in the tones of his growing love-song, excited lust in the comic coloratura, shortness of breath in the hurried rhythm, and finally the only humanly sincere excitement in the reeling dance-melody of the Bacchus duet. The possibilities of the grotesque bass, representing the man who has passed his manhood, are completely exhausted in this one type.

A descendant of Osmin, though but an episodic figure, is the gardener Antonio in FIGARO: but there are more important connections between Osmin and Leporello. Leporello is, to be sure, not much interested in love. His need for women is limited to little pranks. Woman as such plays no rôle in his life. In money and gastronomic delights he finds the height of a wise man's enjoyment. In a way, he corresponds, among the servants, to the laughing philosopher Alphonso, in COSÌ FAN TUTTE. The aria in which Leporello reads off the roll of Don Giovanni's loves shows that Mozart thought of him chiefly as representing a cynical outlook on mankind, and only incidentally as a comic figure. Otherwise Leporello would be a *tenore buffo* rôle, and no such rôle exists in DON GIOVANNI. As a *tenore buffo,* Leporello would have had to be a jester, whereas Mozart gives him beautiful music to sing. Leporello is a poor devil who does not know the luxury of fantasy, and therefore sees mankind and the world without illusion, as they really are. The fact that this outlook belongs to a servant is what gives the character its involuntary humor: Leporello is a cousin of Sancho Panza. Thus to the flattest text he sings an expressive Mozart *cantilena,* and he has to be a bass, because comic effect in a vocal characterization comes only through contrast. Thus in Leporello the bass voice is made to represent the activity of a busybody, while in the Commander it represents almost lifeless peace and unearthly loftiness.

But the figures of Osmin, Leporello, the Commander, and to a certain extent Alphonso, are only on the periphery of the world of Mozart's male voices. They serve as contrast, and thus their function, as character types, is indirect. Truly masculine force and active personality are embodied in Figaro and Sarastro: the one, viewed realistically, in his cunning alertness; the other, mythically conceived, in his dignity and wisdom. That Sarastro must be a bass, because of his generally paternal character, was clearly indicated. But his growth into a princely character, into the priest-king, was the result of Mozart's vocal characterization, which brought forward the fundamental significance of the bass voice while it emphasized its melodic possibilities. It is just this melodic treatment of the bass that makes Sarastro move.

Everything in Mozart is unprecedented and unique, it is true; yet the uniqueness of his use of the bass voice is particularly noteworthy. There were many bass rôles written after him, mostly fathers' or character parts, but they are all of secondary significance. No one ever succeeded again in creating central characters with bass voices. Only Mozart wrote these two thoroughly contrasted parts: Sarastro, who embodies the solemn repose and the melodic power of the bass; Figaro, who illustrates its agility, its versatility, and above all its rhythmic vitality. Just as with Leporello, the effect created by Figaro is based largely upon the contrast between the liveliness of the music he sings and the dark timbre of his voice, which is firmly rooted in masculinity. The tenor voice in this part would have raised the especially virile portions to a high pitch of heroic pathos which was far from what Mozart desired. It would have been contrary to his purpose to have allowed moments like the "Non più andrai" to be translated by loud and brilliant singing into a lofty sphere. They must remain on a natural plane. And they could remain on that plane only if sung by the natural (that is, the darker) male voice. The man whom that voice mirrors is a realist for whom all doubts are resolved.

The courting, desiring, conquering man, the man of never-ceasing passion, is represented by a third group. To this group belongs the voice that is closest to man's nature: the baritone. It combines the force and the satiated virility of the bass with the lighter coloring of the tenor register. The baritone can take on a languishing and coaxing character, without giving up its fullness and passion. It thus combines the tenderness of the lover with the brutality of the lord and master. It is the true incarnation of the male sex. Mozart creates three embodiments of this conception: Almaviva in FIGARO, Don Giovanni, and Papageno.

They are three versions of a single basic conception. Though completely contrasted as personalities, they represent in their variety a triple division of a conception of masculinity which would not have been plausible

W. A. Mozart

if embodied in a single human character. At the same time, each displays individually a versatility, an iridescent changeability, which gives it the stamp of complete reality. Almaviva is the most dependent upon the outer world, inclined to slyness and deception, only to return in the end—apparently, but incredibly—to conventionalism. His true nature breaks through unadorned only once, in the big aria: "Vedrò mentr'io sospiro." His slyness displays itself all the more in his sudden transitions from domineering mastery to coaxing gallantry, from impetuous rage to *grandezza* worthy of his station. Almaviva is the hardest part in all Mozart for the singer to impersonate. There is something unyielding about it—in contrast to everything else in the work—which is simply not to be overcome. As full of life and movement, as ready for action as the character appears, it never achieves a leading part in the action, and the effect of the total suffers through the fact that it is the Count at whose expense the entire action proceeds.

Don Giovanni is altogether different. The Don is unceasingly true to his formula of insatiable passion. Thus he makes use of occasional bits of cunning for specific purposes, but any consistent deception or self-denial, in the style of the Count, would be impossible for him. His path leads straight from the first to the last scene. The complete unity of his character keeps one from taking anything quite seriously that would conflict with or hinder the achievement of his goal. Don Giovanni would be a diabolic figure if he did not sing so beautifully. His singing is his justification. In his singing is the specific and only possible explanation of Don Giovanni, in whom is embodied a basic type not alone of opera but of all art. Just as the figure of Faust could be made clear only through the media of speech and thought, so Don Giovanni could come to life only through the voice. It is the voice that makes it possible to give artistic expression to the secret of Don Giovanni's nature, the irresistibility that is rationally unexplainable, the spell he casts. He displaces all moods with the infatuating spell of his manly voice, in which is contained all the sensuality of strength.

In a similarly straight line, but on a different, more primitive level, runs Papageno's course. In him, man as a creature of sex is formulated in the simplest terms: the sex impulse as such reigns in purest naïveté. Thus Papageno is the only German-speaking figure among the three virile male characters. He cracks jokes, and loves to eat and drink. His music is the melodious tinkling of bells, and merry prattle. The ideal towards which it aims is the mating call of nature's creatures, and it ends in a phallic dance-duet joyously celebrating prospects of reproduction without limit.

With these three great baritone figures, Mozart arrived at a final approach to nature as regards the male sex, just as the Countess, Susanna, Elvira, Zerlina, and Pamina reveal the secret of the female voice. The male figures are both more numerous and, each within himself, more versatile than the female, for which after all only one type of voice was at Mozart's disposal. But, as a matter of fact, what they all have to say is expressed only partially in their solos. The most important parts occur, not in the arias, but in the concerted numbers.

In Gluck, ensembles of soloists occur only to a limited extent, as duets and trios, in which, however, interweaving and contrast of the voices hardly enters at all. For intensification and contrast Gluck uses the chorus. But in Mozart's works the chorus—like the ballet, which, apart from the little Fandango in FIGARO, is not found in his chief operas—plays hardly any rôle. FIGARO, too, is the only one of the three Italian operas that contains a choral episode. In the ENTFÜHRUNG there is a little choral music, used for purely illustrative purposes. Only the ZAUBERFLÖTE has, at the end of both finales, short but weighty choral passages, and, in the course of the second act, those choruses of the priests, which are termed a counterpart of the women's choruses in Gluck's IPHIGÉNIE EN TAURIDE. But even these choral movements are solemn points of repose rather than elements of the action, which in Mozart remains for the most part restricted to the interplay of the solo voices.

While this interplay exhibited all phases of personality, in the greatest possible variety, it necessarily made the mutual interrelations of the personalities concerned the chief object of the action. Thus the solo vocal character grew into a member among equal members of a chamber-work for voices. The personal thing about them was expressed only in the associations of the personalities with one another, in their coming together, their concerted singing, their flight from one another. This is true even in the duets. Thus the really deceptive effect of Giovanni's "La ci darem" becomes clear only when Zerlina's answer is heard.

Here the most striking structural differences present themselves between Mozart's German and Italian operas. The Italian operas are built towards a sextet-climax, combining three women's and three men's voices. This sextet, which determines the design of the finale in all three works, is prepared by duets, trios, and quartets, made up of different vocal combinations, and in the course of the finale itself it is enlivened by gradual confluence of the voices and the occasional elimination of individual voices. It sums up, to a certain extent, the work's entire sphere of action, in which the separate forces come together, fused by the guiding purpose into the higher organism.

Neither of the German operas attains the streaming vitality of these Italian finales. Except for the quintet in DIE ZAUBERFLÖTE, in which the three women's voices (which must be considered as a unit) are combined with Tamino and Papageno, none of the ensembles in the German operas exceeds the quartet. In DIE ENTFÜHRUNG, Mozart employs the simplest combination: two women's and two men's voices—in fact, two sopranos and two tenors. In DIE ZAUBERFLÖTE the combinations are fewer: a short quartet passage for four women's voices (Pamina with the Pages), a quartet for soprano, two tenors, and bass (Pamina and Tamino with the Men in Armor), together with trios of various sorts. None of these passages is comparable, for significance of structure, to the Italian ensembles. Their effect is simply to confirm things which have already been brought out in the dialogue. Even the two great finales of DIE ZAUBERFLÖTE show, despite their dimensions, chiefly the desire to avoid the interruption of music by dialogue. They are put together in medley fashion, in contrast to the unified, organic form of the Italian operas.

These differences in the form of the ensembles are based upon the differences between the languages. The Italian ensemble, with its maze of interweaving voices and its ever-changing contrast of the various groups, would have been impossible in German from the point of view of both song and text. So for clarity's sake, if for no other, Mozart had to choose a simple form of *lied*-like concerted singing. Reason enough why he could not renounce the possibilities of Italian opera, for which, besides, he had better trained singers at his disposal.

Hence the differences, too, in the types of subject dealt with in German and Italian texts.

3

The subject matter, to judge from the outside, seems primary, and may be so in the historical course of the individual case. Seen in its proper relations, however, it is effect, not cause. The fundamental consideration is the human type which, according to the outlook of the time, it is possible to attach to each particular vocal type. Mozart's vocal types are of two classes: society characters and fairy-tale characters. Fairy-tale characters are figures completely unencumbered by convention, following only their own impulses; society characters are figures who remain in continuous conflict between convention and natural impulse. This is the basis of the difference between Pamina and the Countess, Papageno and Don Giovanni, Sarastro and Figaro, Osmin and Leporello. It is the fundamental difference between Mozart's German and Italian operas. One might say in this connection that Mozart conceived the singing voice in two different ways: as the German voice and as the Italian voice. The German voice manifests itself in the individual creature of feeling, the bearer or the symbol of an idea. The Italian voice manifests itself in the creature of society, revealing itself as an individuality only in its relations with others.

Hence there arise two worlds of subject matter: Italian society plays and German folk plays.

Society plays are studies of character and of the times. Their proper frame is the present—temporal and spiritual realism, as in FIGARO or COSÌ FAN TUTTE. In them the play of social situation and conversation can freely unfold—the naturalism of the ensemble is given. They are not, to be sure, conditioned upon realism. In the case of a character-piece, like DON GIOVANNI, time may be turned back, realism may be mixed with elements of mysticism. The goal of the Italian operas is the revelation of the essentially human, hidden behind the disguises and masks of society. The human being is exposed down to the root of his nature, to the point where he can go no farther by himself and either, like the Count, prays for forgiveness; or, like Giovanni, reaches everlasting damnation; or, like the people in Così, arrives at a clear recognition of man's insufficiency. As intellectual matters, these are works not of naïve but of highly critical content, in which the characters are not, to be sure, individualized on the *leit-motif* system, but revealed, as it were, as the curtain of melody goes up. The essential thing, therefore, is always that the style of performance should suit the fluency of the Italian *parlando* and the singing quality of the Italian *arioso.*

The German operas run a different course. In them it is the main concept that determines the style of performance. Love and Freedom in DIE ENTFÜHRUNG; Love, Freedom, and, highest of all, Wisdom in DIE ZAUBERFLÖTE—these are the goals of the two operas mentioned. The tale is fundamentally the same in both works: the captive princess, the youthful liberator, the clear-seeing and self-denying Pasha (the latter serving, in DIE ENTFÜHRUNG, as the first sketch—its development arrested before it got further than dialogue—for the figure of Sarastro). These are the basic impulses. The tale and the development of the action in DIE ENTFÜHRUNG remain very shortwinded. DIE ZAUBERFLÖTE, on the other hand, is richly endowed. Just as it combines singing voices in all the forms in which they appear in the German operas, and adds the chorus as an important structural element, so it develops its subject matter to a culmination of its possibilities. Out of the interplay of personalities, idealized into bearers of symbols, there develops the legend of music, of the power of tones. Music tames wild animals, restrains evil men, conquers fire and water, brings forth a Prince for the Princess and a little wife for the little man of nature, and leads all humanity through wisdom and virtue to harmony.

It is music that accomplishes all this, for music held, for Mozart, the creative secret of life. Music as creative power, as the force that gives shape and order to things, is, therefore, the content of this work, which, in its ideological impulses, is far from the society drama and personality analysis of the Italian operas. It represents the other hemisphere of Mozart's opera world.

There can never be any thought of comparing these basically different categories. But it should be noticed that the difference between them arises from the different ways in which Mozart regarded the singing voice. Beyond all differences of character and personality, Mozart's conception is divided by language into German and Italian halves. The two are in themselves equally perfect and, according to the nature of the languages, basically different. Thus both are determined, in their subject-matter and its treatment, by these given points of departure, and from them the creative possibilities are brought to fulfilment.

But untouched by this duality of the creative impulse, radiating in two opposite directions, there remains at the heart of Mozart's creation the concept of the relation of the sexes as the source of all life. "Mann und

Weib und Weib und Mann reichen an die Gottheit an," * sing Pamina and Papageno. Creatures essentially quite alien to each other—the young girl just awaking to romantic love and the primitive man of nature—are brought together in that idea. Its development determines the course of action and thus the whole organic structure of the drama.

That "Man and Woman" should find each other, or lose each other, is the sole significance of the action; all else is present only for the sake of this primary content. Development, in the sense of dramatic action materially more strongly unified, does not come into consideration. Hence the two-part design of the structure. This design does not aim at the dénouement of the drama in the central point of the action, which would have necessitated the three-act form. It consists of a double *crescendo,* leading the first time to the entangling of the threads, the second time to their untangling.

A firm grip on this two-part structure is necessary to a proper representation. It is therefore wrong to alter, for external reasons such as difficulties in scene-changing, the two-part division into a four-part one, as is often done in DON GIOVANNI, or, by making a cut in the second *finale,* to give DIE ZAUBERFLÖTE a three-act form. The scenic architecture must be based on the

* Man and woman and woman and man, [together] they equal gods.

musical. The goal of the latter, in Mozart, is always in the *finale* of the act, for which all the preceding pieces serve as substructure.

The same is true of the scenic form. With the proper arrangements, it is evident that Mozart's conception is always based upon the *finale* to come. The settings of the *finales* of each act are always the most complicated and the most spaciously conceived, whereas the preceding, shorter scenes can always be built into the main, concluding set. This is particularly clear in DON GIOVANNI and DIE ZAUBERFLÖTE. In DON GIOVANNI the first *finale* shows the great feast room with the three ball-orchestras; the second shows Giovanni's dining room, with the appearance of the Commander. Both settings offer space into which the earlier scenes can be built. The same is true in DIE ZAUBERFLÖTE, of which the first act culminates in the great architectural picture of the three temples, while the second ends with the Temple of the Sun. Here the closing scenes are required to be monumental externally as well as in essence, while all the other scenes, Fire and Water included, are short and can change from one to another continuously with a minimum of mechanical rearrangement.

Mozart planned everything quite practically for the theatre. His requirements are equally fulfilled even on a primitive stage. If difficulties arise, they are not to be ascribed to Mozart. He demands neither richness nor unusual pictorial effects—only the feeling of the theatre. A prerequisite is a proper appreciation of time relations, that is, speed and continuity in the succession of the scenes.

Mozart's stage works do not present problems of style, in the deeper sense. When such problems are found in Mozart, it is always at the expense of the sense of the works. The Italian works demand only a realistic frame for the action. In FIGARO and in COSÌ, this frame should be as simple as possible; it should not come to the spectator's consciousness at all as an independent element. DON GIOVANNI permits the imagination more play in respect to color and form. But here, too, the setting is always decoration and any attempt to unveil secrets of style in it is fruitless. DIE ZAUBERFLÖTE, finally, is a real old apparatus-comedy, with trap-doors and elevators, flying-machines, fire, water, animals, and similar magic apparitions. These naïve effects should not be interfered with, especially as the music takes direct cognizance of them, as for example in the A major trio of the pages, who appear in flight.

Furthermore, Mozart's stage must never be made the object of experiments. It remains, even in those passages when the setting is most impressive, a frame for personalities. The most striking example of this rule is the Fire and Water scene in DIE ZAUBERFLÖTE. Mozart does not suggest by a single tone the scenic effect. He has only the march played by a solitary flute, punctuated by the quiet timpani and brass accompaniment. It is not Fire and Water that are to be seen, but Tamino and Pamina.

Thus Mozart is always displaying personalities, and only personalities. He does not scorn the setting: it is important, it is needed, but only as decoration. It is personality that gives it its significance, personality realistically portrayed—no mere figure of the opera world, with easy pathos and threadbare gestures. But not purely a dramatically conceived personality either. FIGARO was originally a play. When Mozart composed it he must have desired to make something else out of it. It would be underestimating Mozart not to be willing to see more in his music than a lovely accompaniment to a drama that good actors could perform without assistance.

Therein lies the problem of performing Mozart: to find singers who can sing the music, and then shape the representation out of the music. The customary manner of performance nowadays is aimed at dramatic naturalism. It regards speech as primary, and attempts, proceeding from that fundamental position, to reconcile song with speech as best it may. This method is sometimes satisfactory enough, or at least not disturbing, when employed by an individual performer; but in the ensemble it leads straight to catastrophe. In the ensembles, the courses of the musicians are exactly plotted, and the relations of the various persons with respect to one another precisely composed, down to the smallest detail. Here the producer who focuses his attention upon dramatic effect has to lay down his weapons and admit their inadequacy, or else use force and destroy the transparency of the musical texture.

These questions of performance are like the task of stage-setting. They are easier to answer than they appear, as long as they are approached without any seeking after mystery. The chief thing to be remembered is that it is not the text, and not the orchestral accompaniment, but solely the singing that gives character to the figure represented. The word, which is always susceptible of many interpretations, receives its special and definite sense from the way in which it is set in the vocal line. The latter alone, then, can determine the nature of the action, and consequently of the gesture as well.

It must also be recognized that the concept of a problem of production was unknown to Mozart. Production that attempts to create anything beyond simple illustration introduces a foreign trait into Mozart's work, and corresponds to arbitrary alteration of the orchestration. The producer can do no more than free the singer for what the music and his conception of the character demand of his performance. Beyond that effort in behalf of the individual, the producer must see to it that the entire performance is as cogent as possible. If he accomplishes these two tasks, he has achieved much. Anything further is undesirable. Mozart can bear it, to be sure, but we are robbing ourselves of his work.

Mozart died at the age of thirty-five. His five chief operatic works were written within the ten-year period from 1781 to 1791. He wrote not only the operas, to which, as an interim work, TITUS must be added. He wrote besides countless other works, for piano, voice, chamber combinations, and orchestra. It would be incorrect to say that these other works are of less importance than the operas. Almost all bear the stamp of genius. But the operas unlocked the widest field for Mozart's talents, and won the greatest popularity for his name. And there is no other domain in which his work remains similarly incomparable. In instrumental music, in vocal compositions, in sacred music, he had both forerunners and successors. To be sure, he remains, even in comparison with them, the only Mozart. But they led the way, and they continued it after him, although with significant differences.

In the operatic field that is not true. Mozart had no successor, any more than he himself had been the successor of Gluck. His work is unique, and complete in its uniqueness; for in it the human voice achieves a perfect realization of its formal possibilities, springing from the most natural basic impulse: love between man and woman.

This achievement took place at the instant when the possibilities of artistic Italian song were still at their zenith, while simultaneously those of natural German song had become capable of artistic exploitation; when the feeling for vocal tone was still alive, and the feeling for instrumental tone already awakened; when linguistic division into national cultures was already a fact, and yet the peaceful existence of the various languages side by side was still possible. It was an instant of rare equilibrium of all material and spiritual cultural elements. At this instant of perfect harmony of all forces, Mozart appears and achieves his work.

From this point on, the streams divide. Languages and stage traditions separate. Man remains no longer a child of nature, simply a character or a personality. He specializes, and develops individual qualities out of the national language or spirit of the language, letting other qualities drop.

For the voice, and thus for the opera, there begins at this point the greatest and most difficult struggle that the operatic form will have to endure—a struggle that calls into question the possibility of its existence: the struggle with instrumental music, the struggle with the orchestra.

Chapter IV

FIDELIO

THE orchestra had already, by the end of Mozart's opera-writing, gone through a series of changes. But the acknowledgment of its subservience to the stage, of its function as accompaniment to the singing voice, had until then remained unchanged. Within these limits there had developed, with increasing freedom, innovations in orchestration, exceptional instrumental solo effects, coloristic solo or ensemble writing. Gluck added to the significance of the orchestra as a dramatic means, and Mozart finally established it.

This more active use of the orchestra was bound to lead gradually to a critical re-examination of the relations between the singing voice and instruments. The singing voice, through its connection with language and with the visual impression of the acting character, had from the beginning the advantage over wordless instruments. It seemed incapable of further development within the opera. At the same time, the expressive possibilities of instruments offered new impulses for dramatic action. Among these possibilities were dynamic contrasts and climaxes. Through intense cultivation of the possibilities of contrast, startling juxtapositions as well as smooth transitions, effects of a nature hitherto unknown had been achieved in symphonic writing. They invited transplantation into the opera. Connected therewith was the exploitation of orchestral coloring. Thematic development as well contributed to the significance of the orchestra. In addition, there was novelty in these orchestral means of expression. The sympathy of both musicians and amateurs turned increasingly towards instrumental conceptions, as was shown by the wide distribution of symphonic music and the tendency in the direction of the concert.

With this preference for instrumental and orchestral music went a lessening of interest in the singing voice. On account of the wider dissemination of music among various classes of society, the fine discrimination that belongs to court-cultures was gradually lost. The singer's art itself declined, on account of the narrowing of the circle of amateurs and connoisseurs. Still more important, man as a creature of nature, portrayable by no other medium as completely as by the singing voice, ceased to be the center of interest. As a result of increasing emphasis upon the force of speech and thought, and of a critical world outlook, a new type of being thrust himself into the foreground: man as a manifestation of intellectual force, the man of ideas. Type had become personality, personality developed into individual character. Out of the individual character there grows now, naturalistic realism being left behind, man as the personification of will and idea.

From this point on the paths of opera divide according to national cultures. The cleavage becomes especially clear in German composition. The naturalistic humanity of Mozart's art disappears and with it goes the simple solution of the problem of opera creation through the singing voice. In place of that all-important medium there enters instrumental music, at first only as a coordinate factor, but gradually achieving primary significance, and finally holding undisputed sway. Connected with this development is the corresponding metamorphosis of the subject matter of the drama from the human to the intellectual.

What, then, is the relation of this development, conditioned by the intellectual history of the period, to the constant nature of the opera as an art-form?

The effort so to combine the German language, German vocal style, German instrumental feeling, and German thought, as to reach the spiritual (not, to be sure, the artistic) level of Mozart's operas was successful in only one work: Beethoven's FIDELIO. For all that it is a unique and isolated phenomenon, FIDELIO is a perfectly valid stage work. Yet, despite its lofty character, it is not in the front rank of Beethoven's achievement. And Beethoven could never make up his mind to write a second opera, although the urge towards opera composition was always in him. Neither occasion, nor incentive, nor desire were lacking; but one obstacle was not to be overcome. What was this obstacle? The impossibility of creating, out of an unvocal language, with the orchestra pressing towards mastery over the voice and the plot determined by intellectual considerations, a work belonging to a species the natural basis of which—the human voice—appeared in it only as a last consideration.

It is not to be assumed that Beethoven saw the problem in that light; he was too thoroughly an instrumental musician. But he was at the same time too critical a craftsman not to recognize the difficulties that resulted. There are sufficient traces of them in FIDELIO, even though Beethoven in the flush of enthusiasm for this first work did not see them. FIDELIO, indeed, shows that one can occasionally instrumentalize the voice, and even at times, under the spell of a transporting idea, idealize it, but that one cannot create an opera without singers. At the same time the strange result is that the voice triumphs in the very place where it is only inserted as an auxiliary force.

Beethoven builds his work upon an instrumental basis. Instrumental music became the factor simplifying and unifying external events, whereas every human element became an added difficulty. Only a musician from whom the overpowering force of his intellectual purpose hid the real meaning of the natural fullness of life could undertake such a task. Beethoven could draw no pure vocal line. The interval-construction of his melodies is determined by instruments, even before they have taken shape, simply because his creative process is the result of abstract tonal imagination and not of the singing impulse. Beethoven's phrases are always unvocal, even when they are apparently constructed with conventional technical means of expression. They are always shaped so as to be least practical for the singer. Even in successful instances, the quality peculiar to the voice emerges only with difficulty.

But this very fact becomes the artistic means which Beethoven employs for his purpose. It would be mistaken to assume that it is due to awkwardness in the ordinary sense. Of course Beethoven could not have written differently, or more gratefully, for the voice; but he would not have done so if he could have. "Do you believe, sir, that I am thinking of your wretched fiddle when the Muse speaks to me?" he answers in a similar situation to Schuppanzigh, when the latter complains to him about a violin figure that is awkward to play. The world of FIDELIO is not that of the opera. But at the same time it is a world governed by strict artistic principles, and must be so regarded. Beethoven withdraws the voice from natural, human song. He makes it clumsy. He neutralizes its sex appeal, even when one would think it should be strongest, as in the introductory scenes of the first act. But all this is in his case inevitable, and profoundly right.

And here, incidentally, are Beethoven's greatest external obstacles. The struggle against the real nature of the opera and its essentially vocal character remains hard, even for Beethoven. According to his intentions, he should have been able to confine himself to the main figures of the action: the tyrant, the innocent sufferer, and the liberating heroine. In them, too, he would have found the three vocal types that he required: the dark baritone for the figure of the oppressor, the high and bright male voice proper for the captive fighter for freedom, and the woman's voice upon which demands are made equally in the high, middle, and low registers.

If Beethoven had had a libretto that permitted this sort of combination, he would doubtless have been satisfied with it. But the plot needed more than this, externally. Means had to be found to set the chief voices properly in motion, and to create contrasts and, above all, new shadings of ensemble tone. FIDELIO is by and large an ensemble opera. Each character, indeed, except

Jaquino and the Minister, has an aria, Pizarro's being written with chorus so that it is clearly brought into the sphere of the action. But these five solo pieces stand over against eight solo-ensembles—duets, trios, and quartets—and also the two finales with chorus.

These are not, to be sure, ensembles which further the action, as in Mozart, where the vocal characters mutually reveal one another. The Beethoven ensemble simply depicts a situation with an express urge towards a sort of concerted conclusion such as one finds in chamber music. The interweaving of the voices is the end sought. At the same time the expressive character of each individual as he speaks may be preserved. Thus in the trio of Leonore, Marcelline, and Rocco, "Gut, Söhnchen, gut," the three personalities are clearly set off against one another, just as in the duet at the grave, in the second act, the nervous prattle of Rocco is set off against the singing lament of Leonore.

But such details have to do with the characterization less of individuals than of situations. Here the latter alone is the determining factor. It leads to such forms as the quartet-canon in the first act, where the four different characters are bound together in the same melodic theme-form: it is not the variety of their personalities, but the unanimity of their agitation that is to be conveyed. As here it is repression, so in the quartet in the second act it is eruption, that is the common feature. Leonore, Pizarro, even Florestan and Rocco, speak in the end the same language. Thematic development rules, the rhythm leaps from one to the other. The voices are working parts of a larger whole, and that whole is fundamentally a piece of music. Would it then be conceivable as such, without staging? No, for the elements of the stage (plot, setting, costume, dramatic situation) are so finely interwoven into the texture of this music that they could not be removed without danger to the sense of the whole. Irrespective of that close connection, however, there remains above all a musical, not a theatrical, creation. The means of singing action are made to serve the ends of musical expression, with the genius's capacity for transmutation.

This is most clearly shown in the two finales. In the definitive version, Beethoven returns to a two-part structure. For Mozart, the Finale (in the Italian operas, that is) is the beginning of the now highly compressed action, so that all that has gone before seems mere preparation. For Beethoven the beginning of the finale closes off the action part of the work, and a broad musical flow sets in.

This is true not alone of the second finale, laid out in true oratorio style, but equally of the first. The apparent interruption through Pizarro's unexpected return and the calling back of the prisoners is an afterthought, a device for rounding out the musical form through the two choral passages. These cantata-like musical numbers have no connection with clarification of the characters or unfolding of the plot. They resemble most closely the finales of DIE ZAUBERFLÖTE, but even compared with these they lack the *quodlibet*-like variety of contrasts. In the finales, Beethoven-the-musician calmly pushed aside the never too plausible Beethoven-the-man-of-the-theatre. Thus two pieces of music of very exalted conception came into being, one of the distinctive features of which is that they are to be performed on the stage with costume and scenery.

This question suggests itself: Is the concept of the theatre really so definitely one-sided that it allows no deviation, no exception, even though sponsored by the most far-reaching genius?

Beethoven's FIDELIO is the greatest example of the impossibility of approaching the theatre from a non-theatrical standpoint, and particularly of trying to form opera out of any other force than the element of the singing voice. Beethoven admired Mozart, but he rejected FIGARO, COSÌ, and DON GIOVANNI because of their subjects. He believed in the possibility of opera as a field for the intellect, as the bearer of ideas. With details that did not suit his purpose and were nevertheless indispensable to the action he tried to effect a compromise. He wanted to lift them into his own sphere, for he needed them.

Thus arose the task of creating a Marzelline, a Jaquino, a Rocco. They were necessary to the outer development of the plot and to the musical development of the ensembles. Thus Beethoven came to the struggle with the original First Act, the struggle of the genius with his material, to which he could find no access, because access was open not to the weigher of ethical values but only to the singing human being. Three times the aria of Marzelline was composed—which does not mean that even in its final form it was singable. Several big ensemble numbers, a duet, and a trio, were written, rewritten, and finally thrown out. Genius worked more industriously and more laboriously than any second-rate talent.

The final version shows that despite all this labor the spiritual level of the score of FIDELIO is not even. To try to smooth it out, as some conductors do, by omitting the Gold aria, for example, is as arrogant as it is useless. Unevenness belongs to this work. It must be recognized and understood.

The three great arias of Pizarro, Leonore, and Florestan remain as complete documents of Beethoven's vocal characterization. All three are acts of violence against the voice. The Leonore aria, besides, received a crack in its stylistic structure through the later prefixing of the big recitative: the figure of Leonore is raised prematurely to a heroine's stature, whereas really it is not until the prison scene that she should achieve the ecstatic force of the heroine. Regardless of this problem, the three arias became determining factors in the history of the German opera that followed. Through an at first conscious over-emphasis of the characteristic element, the heroic vocal types of the soprano, the tenor, and the bass-baritone make their appearance.

Linked with this, the treatment of the orchestra appears especially clear in these three arias, as the real factor that translates the visible stage action, and the words expressing it, into a more sharply precise language, addressed directly to the feelings. The orchestra is confronted with a new task. It is an equal partner of the singing voice and sets off the vital naturalness of the latter against the thought-creating force of instrumental tone. And in so doing, it threatens the independent life of the voice, exposing it to the danger of being choked off by the luxuriant growth of the symphonic organism, and forcing its development under the laws of instrumental line.

At first, to be sure, this confrontation of voice and orchestra takes place in the form not of contrast but of complement. Beethoven himself drew the proper conclusion from his attitude towards opera: in the overture he found the appropriate medium in which to give form to his drama of ideas. That the urge towards this drama of ideas must lead ever further from opera is shown by the history of FIDELIO and its relation to the operas that came after it. The work has always remained an island. Although, thanks to the impetuous force that resides in it, it has established itself upon the stage, it has never really captured the theatre. It was and remains an episode.

The uniqueness of the great achievement remains, as does the problem which this achievement set forth. It showed that the nature of opera gave no creative opportunities to artistic singing in the German language. At the same time, the orchestra was pressing mightily forward, and an instrumental way of thinking and feeling was taking—as a result of the concert, too—firmer and firmer hold upon men's minds. Opera, however, in this older, pompous form, was still fostered for representative purposes, but it had a difficult position to maintain in the face of critical enlightenment. It held on best in the form of the romantic play of enchantment, but it shrank continually into ever smaller forms. That any spiritual impulse should originate here was hardly possible.

A great barrenness fell upon opera. This would have been the time, if ever, to prophesy its decline.

Chapter V

GERMAN OPERA

I

FIDELIO is the only work, of the three decades of German opera composition following Mozart's death, that has survived to the present day. This thirty years' standstill did not arise from a lack of musical talent. It arose from the difficulty of arriving at the necessary new attitude towards opera. The spiritual wretchedness of German opera creation, the undecided marking-time in one dead spot for a period of several decades, was the circumstance prerequisite for the success, unique in the entire history of opera, of Weber's FREISCHÜTZ. Never had there been an expression so widely influential of a national folk-character embracing all classes. With it the musical theatre not only strengthened the foundation that it had almost lost, but considerably broadened it. The opera, which had been simply vegetating, won new life. A new art-form suddenly came into being:

the opera of German romanticism—in short, German opera.

FREISCHÜTZ is a German *singspiel,* made of dialogue and music mixed, similar to ENTFÜHRUNG, ZAUBERFLÖTE, and FIDELIO. Weber, however, does not continue the line followed in those works. He goes farther back, beyond the points of departure of Beethoven and Mozart. The dialogue has a broader scope, is more significant for the action than in FIDELIO and ZAUBERFLÖTE. And within the music, too, it has more importance. This music is simple and transparent in form, primitive and folk-like in its melodic contour and harmonic diction. Weber consequently called down upon himself, from the representatives of aristocratic musical culture, the reproach of dilettantism. Music-lovers of the old school found Weber's folk-nature demagogic, or at least insignificant. What it signified, however, was only that in place of a song-style of Italian origin a new style had arisen, based upon the German language.

Weber's music is in all its elements the result of a productive interpenetration of speech and song. It is the creative determination of how the German singer can and must sing if he wishes not only to form words, but also to illustrate the feelings and concepts that are behind the words. Therefore the melody must be, in line as well as in rhythmic movement, so simple, and at the same time so vigorous, that the meaning of the word comes to life. Therefore the harmonic progressions, apart from numerous instances of imaginative daring, are so completely artless that jaded ears think Weber was not capable of anything better.

How little this is the reason for Weber's musical diction is shown by the treatment of the orchestra and the chorus. But it too could be understood only in relation to the fundamental direction of the new opera. Mozart and Beethoven had created contemporary characters. Even in ZAUBERFLÖTE, where Mozart made use of the form of the legend, the thought and problem content were concerned with contemporary life. The characters of FIDELIO are, to be sure, conceived, in accordance with a predetermined attitude, as idea-bearers. Not only the ideas themselves, however, but the very sphere of life of the whole work, the nature and the action of its members, is directly connected with the period in which Beethoven wrote.

This choice of the contemporary period is no accident. Only in that temporal setting could man naturalistically viewed have his being. This period was so strong, and so naïvely conscious of itself, that the idea never occurred to it to call upon history or mythology, or in any way to consider remoteness from the present as profitable for artistic creation.

Weber's time was different. Starved and disenchanted

through political and cultural stress, its creative forces could find an impulse to creative activity only in connection with the past. Everything spiritual was felt as contrast to reality, and dreaming and flight from the world took the place of the strong realism of the period of Enlightenment. Plot became fantasy, man a creature of the imagination, daylight gave place to the magic of moonlight. Nature itself lost its plastic objectivity and was dissolved in poetic moods. Everything received a conceptual duality, receded into the background, split up into appearance and essence. The world of romanticism took possession of the theatre, and music was its most important handmaiden.

Up to the present day no change has come in the history of the opera to equal in significance the change from the realistic song-opera of the late 18th century to romantic opera. This change was so powerful, and went forward with so little resistance, that, working retroactively, it has even obscured our picture of the older opera. To be sure, romantic opera had really to strive with the same means towards the same conclusion. But its ideology, growing out of the language problem, demanded the setting up of different aesthetic aims.

The humanity of the acting characters no longer arose primarily from their singing: it grew out of the nature of their poetic characterization in words. Accordingly, the vocal types changed from those that had prevailed hitherto. Among the women the young-girl type dominated. It is most impressively represented in the lyric and deeply felt expression of Agathe—Pamina translated into terms of German sentimentality. She is temperamentally complemented by the almost boisterous soubrette-gaiety of Ännchen. They are Weber's two pure German female vocal types. They indicate a uniformity of the German female voice not very fruitful for the stage. That voice remains confined to the expression of tenderness, sauciness, moods of emotional awakening. Agathe and Ännchen may suffice for FREISCHÜTZ, but they would hardly permit of any growth or development beyond its level.

More varied is the treatment of the men's voices. They are written low throughout: even the tenor part of Max, the leading rôle, avoids the high register. Its color is conceived less as lyric than as of manly seriousness, intended for a singer who, with resonant tones in the middle register and good declamation, can get along without a fine or cultivated voice. The fact that the vocal requirements are but half-defined affects the character itself, of course. That so vague and even indifferent a creature as Max could become the central point of a drama shows how far the creative will had strayed into the realm of the fantastic. Tamino, too, undergoes trials (tests directed, incidentally, not at the chance steadiness of his hand but at the strength of his will). Tamino survives, Max is beaten. But Max's failure shows less the unreliability of his character—who, in a desperate situation, would not have done just as he did?—than the inadequacy of the method of testing. And thus the significance of the incident is summed up in the recognition that "zweier edler Herzen Glück" (the happiness of two noble hearts) must not depend "auf einer Kugel Lauf" (upon the course of one ball).

It is a thin moral. It therefore remains in the background, and receives its justification only through the means employed to illustrate it. Among these means, Agathe, Ännchen, and Max take only second rank. The active forces are first Kaspar, then the chorus, and finally the orchestra. With these three forces Weber fashions his new world.

Kaspar is Weber's most imposing character, not alone within DER FREISCHÜTZ. The contrast of this figure with all the others shows how the composer becomes creative the minute he is dealing with a figure who is not content to sing his observations, prayers, or knavish stories, but acts, and acts according to his vocal nature. In this figure the tonal concept "bass" achieves new plastic embodiment. Threads connect him to Osmin, to be sure. But, through the exploitation especially of the deeper coloring, Weber's genius succeeded in advancing one more step the sinister-supernatural type. Sustained tones, as well as uncanny bass coloratura, bass trill, declamatory accents, and finally the melodramatic effect of the spoken word, are inserted for their color value. If there were singers of appropriate stature, the portrayer of Kaspar would crowd all his co-players into the background—so prominently is the part written by Weber. In Kaspar is to be found the essential element of the bass: darkness, power, and diabolic greatness. Even the related figure of Pizarro, though written for a higher register, must yield precedence to him.

Complementing this one figure fully developed in the round is the chorus. As a singing mass it has already been presented in the old opera, serving as a frame, introductory and concluding. Gluck employs it as an important dramatic tonal factor—important through the significant effects of contrast it creates. Even the unusual feature of choruses made up exclusively of men's or women's voices is exploited in IPHIGÉNIE EN TAURIDE and in ZAUBERFLÖTE. Except in the latter, Mozart made little use of the chorus, and Beethoven's FIDELIO choruses, intrinsically important as they are, remain on the periphery of the main action.

In Weber something new occurs. The chorus as a whole, as well as in its division into men's and women's choruses, becomes an atmospheric element of the drama. To the same extent that the leading voices become mixed phenomena, compounded of their speaking and singing natures, the chorus as a singing and acting mass takes on personality. It gathers up and reflects in its bright sound-mirror the entire image of the work. The individual forfeits some of his personal significance. Agathe, Max, Ännchen cannot be compared with Pamina and Tamino, and Kaspar is more an evil principle than a personality. In the background and beneath the surface, however, a new estate has grown up. It takes unto itself what the figures of the foreground yield. It develops it further, gives to the whole a new color, a new depth, a new perspective of sound. It creates, that is, a new musical world of space.

The chorus still appears, of course, as a mass, even where it splits up into men's and women's voices. But this mass does not have the uniform completeness it had in the old opera. It strives towards division into groups, most clearly in the "Viktoria" and Mocking Choruses, as well as in the groups of maidens. The setting loses the stamp of choral writing. The voices are felt as individual values and so treated. The variety of the tasks set it during the unfolding of the action demands from the chorus a versatility which, seen as a whole, gives it the aspect of an individual character.

This is the great reservoir of musical force. In it those sacrifices to speech which are made in the solo-parts were compensated for. In this way, too, it was possible to appease the listeners' need for some resonance in the singing. If the number of solo singers who met the requirements of the old art of song was diminishing, the number of those among the public who were connoisseurs of that art of song was diminishing as well, and thus German choral singing blossomed forth in *Liedertafel* and *Vereine*. Weber himself had given it important stimuli, especially through his "Lyre and Sword" choruses. That part of this movement which carried over onto the stage found among the new opera-listeners the same receptive attitude as Italian cantilena and coloratura had once found among the cultured connoisseurs at court.

In the chorus, German opera struck new roots. In such choruses, no longer stiff and merely accompanying, but now an active element, the bourgeois listener recognized himself. They served the same function in the popularization of the new opera as had once the favorite melodies of the arias. Young girls' singing societies and huntsmen's choruses became the true folk-basis of the FREISCHÜTZ.

The orchestra does not fully correspond to the new creative significance of the choruses. But here, too, the same fundamental shift is to be seen: simplification of (in the old sense) artistic writing in favor of sharper individualization through the exploitation of coloristic means. The wind groups disintegrate into their component parts. Flutes, oboes, clarinets, and horns display themselves, and show the individuality of their character in solo passages. Musical invention is directed at the emphasis of occasional special effects. In the process, instruments are considerably freed for technical agility. The string orchestra receives, through lively figuration, new brilliance, and, through dazzling unison passages, a new virtuoso flair. The FREISCHÜTZ Overture, with its horn-, clarinet-, and cello-soli, its figure work, *tremoli,* and unison passages for strings, and its kettle-drum soli, is a compendium of these effects. Their purpose is always to reveal the color values of the tones of individual instruments, to allow them to make their solo effects, and then to achieve a big dynamic climax through their combination.

Picturesque and color-giving, too, is the treatment of the orchestra throughout the work, although here only the scene in the Wolf's Glen offers opportunity for special orchestra effects. Instrumental soli are continually emerging: in the drinking song of Kaspar it is the piccoli, in Ännchen's humorous account of her dream the solo viola, in Agathe's moonlight aria the clarinet. The fantastic side of the life of nature, which transforms secrets of darkness into elements of the action, determines the whole treatment of the orchestra. It is fundamentally simpler than Mozart's orchestra, and in its instrumentation only slightly augmented. It is not symphonically treated, although many thematic reminiscences appear. *Concertante* brilliance raises the coloristic significance of instrumental tone to highest intensity.

While the orchestra becomes a means of tonal illumination, the entire scenic apparatus serves the purposes of poetic illustration. Here, too, something new is produced through a hitherto unfamiliar manner of giving new intensity to something essentially old. Mozart's Italian operas and FIDELIO got along without unusual scenic effects. ZAUBERFLÖTE, to be sure, was, like all magic plays, a mechanical show, but consciously intended to give the effect, through its highly colored variety, of the improbable, of the legendary in the theatre. But the magic of FREISCHÜTZ is intended seriously. The nature of romantic opera is conditioned upon its being taken seriously. Faith in the theatre, which later became an ethical postulate of romanticism at its height, appears already here, though unexpressed as a prerequisite.

Thus FREISCHÜTZ leads from the theatre into the domain of real spectres. This is even truer of the appearance of Samiel than of the Wolf's Glen scene, for his wanderings in the world of reality are connected with many unpleasant happenings. But it is just as unavoidable as the trial shooting, or the forester Kuno with his lord Ottokar and the hermits. Thus the naïveté of the work must be guarded even in those places where it is as hard for the listener of today to bear as it was for all rationalistic thinkers in Weber's own time. Nothing is to be gained in an attempt to adjust things by stylizing them. Criticism destroys romantic opera, as daylight destroys ghostly apparitions. The further this art stands from actuality the stronger is its demand for the appearance of reality, for the naturalism of the stage, for the magic of artificial being. It may no longer be conscious legend-drama. Everything is the complete illusion of the actual, such as only the theatre can produce.

For the nation, FREISCHÜTZ was not alone the first German opera (made so by its limitations). It was the first typically German play since Schiller's death. When it appeared, the speaking stage was just as impoverished as German opera after Mozart. Nothing was really known of Kleist, and the high tragedies of Müllner and Grillparzer bore too definitely literary features to reach out beyond the circle of cultured readers and achieve genuine popularity. But this immeasurable folk-popularity was the great secret of FREISCHÜTZ. Thanks to it, opera, which had grown rigid with intellectual appeal, or, on the other hand, grown idiotic with magic tricks, now suddenly appeared as the only form of theatrical entertainment that fulfilled all desires. The common denominator for a national audience had been found. For the first time the idea of a people made up of burghers and peasants as a cultural unit came to expression on the stage. This idea was represented not only in the subject matter of the drama, in the prevailing nature-coloring, in the entanglement of the fate of human beings with the secret forces of their environment. It was represented above all in the way in which the German language grew into song. In this opera, which renounced all the fashions of earlier operas, simple song melodies were sung. Through them the people itself, represented in this case by the chorus, became the direct exponent, the special bearer, of the vocal development, and gave it its peculiar breadth of effect.

Zauberflöte was unique; Fidelio was unique; and Freischütz was unique, but even more exclusively so than the other two works. Behind each of these former stood great creative genius, and, to be sure, the deeds of such genius are not patterns from which any desired number of copies may be made. Therein lies a difference between the organic fulfilment represented by the achievement of a man of genius and the single success, made possible by a series of particularly lucky circumstances, of a gifted talent. Such a talent was Weber: no less, but no more. Goethe already points out that in weighing the success of Freischütz the author of the text must not be forgotten. By this remark he meant less to praise Friedrich Kind than to emphasize the particularly lucky combination of external circumstances that attended the success of Freischütz. The course of Weber's own activity confirms this view. The success of Freischütz eggs him on. At the same time he is hurt by critical utterances on the part of his colleagues—among whom are Spohr, Spontini, Grillparzer, and many another serious lover of art—who do not consider Freischütz of great musical importance. Weber attempts to carry over the central idea of German opera into the through-composed form. A commission for Vienna furnishes the occasion, but the result is negative. Euryanthe, greeted with high expectations, is a failure.

The elements of Freischütz are again present: the struggle between good and evil, the attachment of human destiny to a ghostly world filled with secrets. In the musical structure there are solos of every sort from simple songs to big arias. The ensembles, to be sure, are not constructed with any special artistry, yet they show unusual tonal combinations, among which, in the second act, is that of a solo woman's voice singing above the entire male ensemble. Wagner used this combination similarly in the second finale of Tannhäuser, where the figures of the plotting couple with their imposing duet of hate return in Ortrud and Telramund. In addition, there are choruses in great variety, notably a brilliantly written men's hunting chorus, a May song. There is in general so much beautiful music in the work that, if the worth and success of an opera depended upon the content of its music, EURYANTHE should not yield first place even to FREISCHÜTZ.

But this music lacks the most important thing: the folk-element and naïve genuineness. It is like a child of nature who finds himself in a strange sphere of society and vainly attempts to make himself at home. EURYANTHE is the classic example of composed music—of an opera made to fit a certain musico-literary intention. The product of an ambition which considered the folk-work too slight, and which therefore sought to outdo it through cultivated artistry, was bound to fail. Not on account of the text, small as is the pleasure it offers, from the point of view of language. The work was bound to split upon the incompatibility of the composer's conscious purpose and his own fundamental nature, because the task made apparent the limits of Weber's gifts.

There is, apart from the smaller works written before FREISCHÜTZ, still a third work of Weber, which has maintained itself upon the stage, although under many limitations, until the present day: OBERON. It was written for a commission from London. The form was largely determined by that fact, for Weber could no longer produce a German work. In the version that survives, OBERON goes back even farther than the *Singspiel* type represented by FREISCHÜTZ. Large ensembles are entirely lacking. One genuinely powerful dramatic scene, that of Rezia, stands alone. Simple little songs, instrumental Intermezzi, above all choruses, kept to modest dimensions and of great musical charm, make up the greater part of the score. Interest in the staging dominates to such an extent that apart from the magnificent virtuoso overture only Rezia's "Ocean, thou mighty monster" juts up like a gigantic and solitary boulder from the plain. At the same time, in the smaller pieces in OBERON Weber struck precisely the popular note, unspoiled by excessive artifice, of the German oriental tale. This new appeal is apparent particularly in the tonal portrayal of the elfin world. And it doubtless accounts for the ever repeated attempts to adapt OBERON successfully to the German operatic stage.

2

The cause of Weber's failure after FREISCHÜTZ was the false effort to raise the folk-opera, considered not artistic enough, to the plane of a supposedly higher art-form. But, even apart from that false evaluation, would a continuation of the FREISCHÜTZ line have been in any way possible? The question may appear useless, since the one man who would have been able to answer it, Weber himself, avoided it instead. Perhaps that extraordinarily clear-thinking, wise, and intellectually well-rounded man did not believe in the possibility of fruitful continuance on the plane of FREISCHÜTZ, and consequently sought his way to the through-composed EURYANTHE. But why should it not have been possible for Weber to achieve further successes after FREISCHÜTZ, and, in a similar direction, like those achieved by the considerably more limited Heinrich Marschner, with VAMPYR and TEMPLER UND JÜDIN and, above all, HANS HEILING?

In these works, to be sure, the folk-quality, particularly in the men's choruses, often has the character of the most insipid *Gesangverein* music, and the plot inclines more and more to stuffy, ghost-story romanticism. But Marschner, who seems so thoroughly philistine in his lighter moments, shows an astonishing power of invention the minute he turns his attention to nocturnal phenomena, to visions of demonic grotesqueness. In this respect he surpasses Weber, and, in fact, succeeds in creating new character-types in the realm of gruesome fantasy.

The element of predestination to suffering, of dependence on fate, of control by invisible and intangible forces, pushes its way through to musical illustration. The impulse in that direction was the impulse of the man who sees the world not as round and smooth, but with innumerable obscurities and backgrounds, and who would like to act but is powerless to do so. That man, controlled by spirit, or by his destiny, or by some other extra-human force, becomes the new moral center of the romantic opera. Kaspar was already such a man, but his Samiel had an independent existence outside Kaspar himself. Marschner's newly created man carries his destiny within him. He is no longer a villain; he is a marked man, the man of foreordained suffering: the romantic human being.

Even this new man has, as a vocal phenomenon, forerunners in the old opera. Closest to him is Gluck's Orestes, but Don Giovanni, too, has similar features, as do Pizarro and Lysiart. This has always been the type of the most masculine men. But only now, as a result of the disclosures of the romantic spirit, is it possible to delineate it clearly and definitely: it is the baritone type. It embraces, except for the extreme reaches, both high and low tones. At the same time it possesses the full strength, as well as the full tenderness and agility, of the male voice. It is, therefore, the voice of the most characteristic and forceful expressive values. As such it was bound to become prominent as soon as the special, purely vocal effects produced by high and low tones were less in demand than the normal, and therefore best-sounding, middle register.

This voice-type, the heroic baritone, Marschner was the first to place consciously in a central position. To be sure his Vampyr, his Templar, his Heiling still bear many lyric traces, but the dominating character of the baritone, as such, is already present. It prescribes the fundamental color of the work and the relations of the character in question to the other active forces. In respect to these latter, certainly, Marschner remains within well-worn grooves. Thus his works are really beginnings which, though full of genius, were never brought to their proper conclusion because of the adoption of conventional elements. None of his operas is nearly as well-rounded as DER FREISCHÜTZ; none shows a concentration approaching that of DER FLIEGENDE HOLLÄNDER. With the intuitive realization of the new romantic vocal type, and with its embodiment in three great figures, Marschner's work was achieved. Yet there was still lacking not only a new force, but above all new dramatic impulses. For these, however, it was necessary to tap other sources besides those offered by German romantic opera.

3

Retrospective observation allows us to see historical development laid out as a systematically organized course of events. One part fits another—the observer need only place occasional boundary posts to mark period divisions, so that historical articulation may be preserved.

But in reality things happen very irregularly. "Time" is a fitful creator, spasmodic and unpredictable. It is like a volcano, counted extinct until it suddenly produces an eruption more violent than any that ever preceded it.

That is the way things happened in the German romantic operas that now followed. History, as it is usually related, counts Louis Spohr's FAUST, which was produced in 1816, as their first representative work. But to consider Spohr as a romantic is, despite occasional external connections, inaccurate. As an artistic phenomenon Spohr stands between two periods. It is not exoticism or spookiness, nor yet chromatic writing and enharmonic changes, that distinguish the musical romanticist. These things belong, it is true, to the characteristics that determine his style. But the decisive element is the urge towards a genuine folk-character, towards the emphasis of national characteristics in landscape, in temperament, in thought. The essentially new thing in romantic opera was not this or that stylistic feature. It was the fact that the old concept of art was dissolved and a new type of genuinely popular stage work was set up with the aid of German song. This stage work spoke not only from the heights of Sarastro to the people. It played in the midst of the people and was sung forth by that very people as its own and out of its own experience.

This was true of Weber and Marschner, but not of Spohr, who is incorrectly considered the third member of their group. He belongs, rather, to the posterity of

Mozart, to the world of the 18th century. The series of new-type, romantic operas shows that all the important examples of this species occurred within twelve years, between 1821 and 1833. FREISCHÜTZ appears in 1821, EURYANTHE in 1823, in the same year as Spohr's JESSONDA, OBERON in 1826, VAMPYR in 1828, TEMPLER in 1829, HANS HEILING in 1833. At this point the line suddenly breaks off. Marschner, to be sure, goes on composing, but he is no longer able to maintain the level of HEILING. Ten full years pass before the appearance of the work in which the HEILING line is taken up and developed to a new goal: DER FLIEGENDE HOLLÄNDER. Into this ten-year gap, however, there creeps another group, also growing on romantic soil, developing the old *Singspiel* but in a less pretentious way: the comic opera of Albert Lortzing.

It fits the interval between HEILING and the HOLLÄNDER as well as if it were specifically designed as a sort of recreation-intermezzo. Two years after HEILING, in 1835, came DIE BEIDEN SCHÜTZEN; in 1837 there follows ZAR UND ZIMMERMAN; in 1842, WILDSCHÜTZ. That bridges the time-gap to the HOLLÄNDER, and at the same time fulfills Lortzing's life-task. The two works that came still later, UNDINE (1845) and WAFFENSCHMIED (1846), are mere external elaborations of what had gone before, with no new essential characteristics.

With Lortzing a new being steps into the circle of creative talents. Up until Mozart and Beethoven, the composer had been the musical point of departure and occasionally also the intellectual leader of the performance. But he was not actually one of the executing forces—he stood apart from them. With Weber there comes into being the professional conductor type, the organizing, and in an inclusive sense the directing, authority. It is not only the performance that he leads. He determines the intellectual bearing of the entire institution, attempts to arouse the public through newspaper writings, carries on controversies, and writes on general matters of current interest. The theatre as a public institution becomes the object of consideration, pedagogic questions arise—the repertory is tested. All this hangs together with the romantic urge toward folk-opera, as an institution which even so far as its organization is concerned is rooted in the whole people. Beginning in opera with Weber, Marschner, Nicolai, and simultaneously in concert with Spohr and Mendelssohn, the new type of director develops in all the successors of these men until it finds in Wagner its comprehensive fulfilment.

Beside this evolution a variant arises in the figure of Albert Lortzing: the conductor who takes part in the singing and acting—the singing mime, who writes, composes, acts, sings and conducts. A Shakespeare of

the opera—pocket-size, to be sure, but in his own field fit for any task. This phenomenon is the more remarkable since talents of the sort are particularly rare. E. T. A. Hoffman had essayed a similar achievement, but his gifts were not broad enough and the literary element outweighed the others. Lortzing came up from beneath, from the ranks of the craftsmen. From the position of actor and singer he rose continuously, until he stood on the podium holding all the strings in his hand, and produced his own comedies, just as later Richard Wagner did. The latter, it is true, never practised the profession of singing-actor, but he had mastered it, and created out of his knowledge of it, so that he was able to pick up Lortzing's tracks in this direction.

Lortzing's type of activity was not only a historical curiosity; it determined a new and special type of romantic opera: the comic play-opera. The singing-actor was its point of departure, long and well tried in the performance of Italian and French *buffo* operas. His attempt now was to enlarge the modest form of the German *Singspiel* through the adaptation of these foreign models, and, in addition, to draw in the orchestral and choral innovations of romantic opera and relate them to this gay entertainment-art. The idea of the folk-work, as it had been conceived in a serious, aspiring way in FREISCHÜTZ, was now translated into the *buffo* realm.

Only a man of the theatre could set himself that task and accomplish it as successfully as Lortzing. Here there was no help to be gained from ideas. Everything depended upon the realization of the dramatic effect. If this missed fire everything was lost. The homely but hopeless primitiveness of the older *buffo-Singspiel,* like Dittersdorf's DOKTOR UND APOTHEKER or Schenk's DORFBARBIER, shows the distance that separates them from Lortzing's achievement. It was possible to him only by virtue of the fact that he, himself a singing-actor, received his really productive stimuli on the stage itself.

The effect of stage and action were for him the kernel. Around them grew the musical form, the melodic expression. The series begins with the charming but musically and dramatically still limited opera-*Singspiel,* DIE BEIDEN SCHÜTZEN. In glorious freshness of invention and power there follows the folk-opera ZAR UND ZIMMERMANN. Closely connected with it is the *buffa,* WILDSCHÜTZ, already of considerable subtlety, bordering on the sphere of FIGARO. This series shows how the music grows out of the ever richer unfolding of dramatic talent, how this growth of the music is really only a subsidiary phenomenon to the dramatic gift, which, in turn, receives the impulse to expand from its connection with music and the possibilities of song. Lortzing in his acting and singing is always getting deeper and deeper into music. And the works after WILDSCHÜTZ, too, show how he is being gradually sucked down into the vortex of music. And thus he comes into regions for which his gift for the theatre no longer offers him the help he needs, so that in UNDINE and REGINA the flood of music closes over him, and no longer receives its form from the dramatic impulse.

Nevertheless, this modest professional singer gave the German stage four works that are still alive today and of which the artistic directness and spontaneous growth always delight anew. In them he established the dramatic types that were really suited to the nature of the German language and of German singing possibilities. The fact that in all this he to some extent followed Italian models cannot be counted a weakness in him since it is pardoned in Mozart. Moreover, Lortzing never simply followed his models—the *buffo* basses —but always elaborated on them. But he was the first German opera-composer after Mozart to conceive his stage-figures in terms of definite vocal types, and to embody each of these various types in a series of individual and separate examples. This Weber did only in respect to the chorus, and Marschner only in respect to the romantic heroic baritone. Lortzing, the naïve comedian, conjures forth a whole family.

He begins with himself as the simpleton tenor-buffo Peter, in DIE BEIDEN SCHÜTZEN. In the Peter Iwanow of ZAR UND ZIMMERMANN, in the Görg of SACHS, in the Veit of UNDINE, up to the Görg in WAFFENSCHMIED, he develops this line, which reaches its conclusion in Wagner's David. Besides the tenor-buffo, and soon outweighing him in dramatic importance, there enters the bass-buffo. He is the real comedian of the opera: a high bass, with a flexible voice—the bumpkin, the man who always knows better, and yet usually ends up in the rôle of the bamboozled Punch, the pot-bellied father- or uncle-type. Beginning with Schwarzbart in DIE BEIDEN SCHÜTZEN, he achieves fulfilment in one jump in the rôle of van Bett in ZAR UND ZIMMERMANN. Once more, in the Baculus of WILDSCHÜTZ, he finds a perfect incarnation, only to disappear after filling two further posts, jolly but no longer so important, as the Kellermeister Hans in UNDINE and the Ritter Adelhof in WAFFENSCHMIED. Apart from these, Lortzing's bass rôles are simply so much vocal filling. In WAFFENSCHMIED alone he created in the humorous father rôle of Stadinger a central character for the singing bass, as a complement to the buffo Adelhof, who, from the musical point of view, is treated too sparsely.

Lortzing also treated with preference the favorite male voice of romantic opera, the baritone. He transformed it into the *bon-vivant* type, the agreeable rake, in a sense a Don Giovanni reduced to Biedermeier proportions, as in Wilhelm of DIE BEIDEN SCHÜTZEN, in

Count Eberbach of WILDSCHÜTZ, in Liebenau of the WAFFENSCHMIED. Throughout, they are bourgeois continuations of Mozart's baritone line, while the Czar, Hans Sachs, and Kühleborn exhibit the romantically masculine conception of this vocal type. The lyric tenor, on the other hand, plays only the rôle of the second lover: in DIE BEIDEN SCHÜTZEN, Wilhelm; in ZAR UND ZIMMERMANN, Chauteauneuf; in the WILDSCHÜTZ, the Baron.

Thus Lortzing exhibits a family of types with many representatives. According to their vocal qualities they fall again into clearly distinguished character groups, within which the most varied individualizations occur. Similarly productive is the group of women's voices. Lortzing avoids, to be sure, the lyric-elegiac Agathe-type. For his early works it seemed perhaps too difficult and at the same time too stale to him, and both Undine and Berthalda bear witness to his embarrassment. His Maries, on the other hand—in the first rank the Marie of ZAR UND ZIMMERMANN, but also the more romantically and very successfully conceived Marie of WAFFENSCHMIED—are, in their happy mixture of freshness, natural roguishness, and restrained tenderness, maidens such as the German stage had not known before. They are the fulfilment of what must have hovered dimly before Weber, but what he did not succeed in realizing, in Ännchen. Among their number, besides the episodic figure of Gretchen in WILDSCHÜTZ, is the superior and ladylike figure, drawn with exceptional lightness of touch, of the Baroness Freimann in the same work, in whom the charm of the soubrette is combined with the elegance of the coloratura.

The last new type is the comic alto. Beginning with the maiden Lieblich, this branch of the family tree includes the barely sketched Widow Brown, the WILDSCHÜTZ Countess with her discreetly desirous maturity, and the old maid Irmentraut of WAFFENSCHMIED, who has become a classic. In these figures Lortzing certainly made the connection with the Marzelline type. But apart from the profitableness of that connection, he tapped a new spring of expression, being the first to exploit the middle and lower registers of the female voice. Thus he pointed the way to possible female characterizations within the opera whose development had results in the direction not only of the comic but also of the strictly serious.

Comparison of the work resulting from an only moderate talent like Lortzing's and a musically much richer gift like Spohr's shows that what is important for the operatic stage is not the fund of so-called specifically musical talent, but the special gift for the theatre. Weber had this gift, too. But ambition tore him out of his actual domain into something he considered higher. That was his undoing; it kept him from carrying on his FREISCHÜTZ work, as, to judge from the example of Marschner, he might have done.

To Lortzing such temptations did not present themselves until he had created his chief works. Thus his belated excursion into the land of romanticism could no longer endanger his already completed work. His purpose in the latter had been the setting up for German opera, out of the song-possibilities of its music and its voices, new dramatic types, new dramatic tasks, new dramatic goals. Many men of serious intentions occupied themselves with the recognition of that purpose. But to none of them was it given to find a solution as well compounded of the comedian's sense, of artistic modesty, and of the power of musical characterization, as that of Albert Lortzing. Many believed that by making some connection with the French grand opera they could give German opera the required impetus. Others turned first to Italian opera and only afterwards to Paris. One there was who had also turned to Italy, but had then about-faced towards German opera again, created his masterpiece in Germany, produced it, and a few weeks later died. This was Otto Nicolai.

4

The appearance of Nicolai complements that of Weber. Like Weber, Nicolai leads a restless life, especially in his youth; he is a similarly fanatic and intellectually active temperament, an acute conductor, and an educating, ambitious personality, pursuing high aims, a nature made for achievement. His DIE LUSTIGEN WEIBER (Merry Wives of Windsor), produced in 1849, stands at the end of the series of pure German operas, as FREISCHÜTZ stands at the beginning. It makes use of everything that had been learned in the interim, and especially of Lortzing's work. But Nicolai works with more plentiful musical capital, both as to invention and craftsmanship. He brings with him from Italy, above all, the urge to sing, which his work shows much more markedly than that of Lortzing, who proceeded from the point of view of the actor. Lortzing wrote his own texts, except in the case of WILDSCHÜTZ, for which he used a comedy-project of Kotzebue. Nicolai reached out to Shakespeare. The fact that the MERRY WIVES OF WINDSOR was not Shakespeare on his grandest scale fitted Nicolai's wishes perfectly. He needed only the outlines of the figures; their inner animation remained for the composer.

The models for this work were so well defined that they needed only imaginative individualization: among the women, the agile coloratura, Frau Fluth; the contrasting color of the mezzo, Frau Reich; the tender maidenly tones of Anna; among the men, Fluth and Reich as baritone and bass—the former as the jealous lover, with exceptional vocal flexibility. In addition, a lyric tenor in the lover's rôle, confined, as in Lortzing, to the upper registers; and two *buffi,* Spärlich and Cajus, as tenor and bass. Finally, Falstaff as the chief and central character, less a *buffo* than a humorous character-bass, a good-natured grandson of Osmin, like him familiar with all the arts of singing, and treated somewhat more fully in the lower registers than *buffo* basses usually prefer.

All the characters sing in German, but their creator knows Italian articulation. He gives them a melodic line of such freedom, a *parlando* of such lightness, that the listener notices with astonishment how well the German language is learning to sing. Which demonstrates that under clever management it can very well lay aside its roughness and sound vocal without losing any of its clarity.

But Nicolai is not satisfied with the solo voice. He is again writing ensemble-opera: the first German ensemble-opera since FIGARO. Lortzing, too, wrote many ensembles. But either they incline to the setting of the voices against each other, and are thus limited to dialogue character, or else they rest purely upon the effect of harmonic euphony, as in the men's sextet in the second act of ZAR UND ZIMMERMANN. Nicolai writes the free and yet always confluent chamber ensemble that bears the stamp of Mozart, such as Lortzing had in mind in the WILDSCHÜTZ. He also shows the capacity of the German voice for springing back and forth within the play of the voices, for musical conversation, and for nimbleness in repartee and in light dalliance. Nicolai cared more for the interweaving of the voices than for their individual quality. Only Anna and Fenton, the lover-pair, have each a solo scene; everything else is taken care of in ensembles, while the dialogue is treated with noticeable scantiness.

And the solo-ensembles are supported by choruses such as Lortzing, in all his upright straightforwardness, could not write. These are choruses which in color go back beyond Marschner to the legacy of Weber in OBERON. The nature of the orchestral treatment, too, in contrast to the thickness of Marschner's instrumentation or the homemade quality of Lortzing's, resembles Weber. The poetry of tone-color enters once more into its rights, and the orchestral solo receives new poetic significance. There are orchestral effects, like the beginning of the Overture, that need not fear comparison with Weber and Mendelssohn.

Disturbing from the standpoint of dramatic economy is the similarity in treatment of the first and second Finales, the first having, as a matter of fact, the advantage of choral intensification. Disturbing, too, is the composer's turning to an elaborate ballet in the second act. In fact, the whole second half of the work shows something of a let-down. The nature of the treatment is established up to the first half of the second act, with its classic *buffo* duet of men's voices. But from this point on the inner urge of the work slackens. Was it the text he had chosen, or the composer's own lack of buoyancy that was at fault? But even such a lack must be regarded as something higher than a simple failing. It could, therefore, detract as little from the folk-character of this truly extraordinary work as the fact that four decades later Verdi took the same material as the basis for a libretto.

With Nicolai's Lustigen Weiber the history of the pure German—that is, the romantic—opera closes just as definitely as it began with Weber's Freischütz. The works of this art-form grow out of the artistically, culturally, and sociologically conditioned urge towards the reconstruction of opera into folk-opera based on the German language. This reconstruction could not—as Mozart still could in his German *Singspiel* operas and Beethoven in Fidelio—proceed from the same general foundation as the opera that had come before. It had to build the new musical folk-work right up from the bottom out of the simplest dramatic elements of the folk-stage. The work that had to be accomplished in order to make the German language singable and appropriate to the changing expression of the stage, may be compared with the work that had been necessary almost a century earlier in order to adapt the German language to literary expression and render it entirely adequate as a language of literature.

In the course opera took from FREISCHÜTZ to DIE LUSTIGEN WEIBER, this task was achieved. Everything musical and singable that was latent in the German language was brought out into the daylight in the forms of the romantic, the fantastic, the comic, and the fantastic-comic opera. The romantic element in it again became, as a result of the plot alone, a tongue-in-cheek device. Nicolai still wrote, to be sure, genuine elf-music, but his elves were simply people dressed up. Enchantment became mere masquerade. At the same time the possibilities of pure German opera in respect to subject matter were pretty well exhausted. Later works based on these models—Cornelius' BARBIER VON BAGDAD, Götz's DER WIDERSPÄNSTIGEN ZÄHMUNG, Wolf's DER CORREGIDOR—added nothing essentially new.

But German opera had overcome the great stagnation of the period after Mozart, and had demonstrated its possibilities. It had now gained such inner strength that it could afford to look about at the state of foreign production. This looking around, and the reciprocal effects that resulted from it, were not to be avoided, particularly since German opera production fed and lived upon the ideas much more of foreign than of domestic production. Among the former, it was Italian opera which, naturally, still predominated—sung no longer in Italian, it is true, but in German translation—which is not nearly so good.

Chapter VI

OPERA BUFFA AND OPÉRA COMIQUE

WHILE in Germany the fight over national opera was raging, while in France opinions about opera were sharply divided, no such problems were known in Italy. There was no battle of aesthetic theories, no opposition between national and international art-forms. There was, in fact, no opera-problem at all. There could be none. For the problem of opera always has its roots in the relations between song and the spoken language. And Italian had been and remained the mother-tongue of opera.

Thus Italy, even up to the present day, is the only country where such opera wars as the struggle over Gluck in Paris, or the struggle over Wagner in Germany, have never taken place, while opera-production has always flowed steadily on. To the extent that changes did take place, they occurred organically—almost unnoticed, like the change of the seasons. In contrast to the Frenchmen and Germans of the 18th and 19th centuries, Italian composers never occupied themselves as writers, and Italian writing about art never concerned itself with the opera, at least so far as a critical or reforming approach was concerned.

But the artistic understanding of Italian musicians and critics is not for that reason to be counted unimportant. Verdi's letters show the earnestness of his reflection. And such earnestness must undoubtedly have been present in earlier composers as well. Critical intuition shows perhaps greater sensitivity in Italy, among all classes of society, than in any other musical country. And this critical intuition is at all times based on the norm of human song. Any deviation from that basic concept is hardly to be imagined.

Italian opera made up for its devotion to this ideal by sucking into itself all the musically creative forces of the nation, leaving to other vocal music only a smaller portion of those forces, and to purely instrumental music only a trifling remainder.

Although Italian opera remained at first untouched by events in Germany and France, its later reactions show that it was not immune to contagion. Italy lost its significance as the schoolroom for foreigners, who had formerly obtained their education there and then cultivated Italian opera internationally. This resulted in a further reaction. Old Italian opera had appeared under two heads: *seria* and *buffa.* The *seria* was in demand in every theatre in the world; it was the compendium of all the arts of song. The *buffa* began as a subsidiary phenomenon, in fact an entr'acte for the *seria,* and was a popular affair as regards both plot and fundamental musical approach. For this reason it is really closer than the *seria* to the Italian audience.

To the same extent that national opera rose up in other lands, the *buffa* grew in Italy to be the popular representative of operatic composition. What had to be laboriously conquered in other lands arose unconstrained in Italy, blessed with the natural language of song, through exclusion of foreign elements and the consequent coming to the fore of native powers. These forces brought the *buffa* to a perfection which in turn set an example to the outside world. In Germany, to be sure, the *Singspiel* had so firmly established itself on its own account that Italian influences were confined to matters of form. In France, however, the *buffa* was consciously taken over as a model. The scheme of its development leads through the French *Singspiel* to the French national opera-species: the *opéra comique.*

The development and expansion of the *buffa* in Italy itself took place through a few works, of which the greater part still live upon our stage. This development began with Pergolesi's SERVA PADRONA, first performed in 1733. LA SERVA PADRONA is the oldest work in the operatic repertory of today. It is, moreover, the soil from which the family trees of Italian and French *buffo* operas grew. In Italy the most significant of its descendants are Paisiello's BARBIERE (1780), Cimarosa's IL MATRIMONIO SEGRETO (1792), Rossini's BARBIERE (1816), and Donizetti's DON PASQUALE (1843).

The French line begins with Rousseau's LE DEVIN DU VILLAGE, written in 1752, as a direct consequence of the SERVA PADRONA, and passes through *Singspiele* by Duni, Philidor, Monsigny, Grétry, and Isouard, to the chief works of the opéra comique: Boieldieu's LA DAME BLANCHE, Auber's FRA DIAVOLO, and Adam's LE POSTILLON. Then they melt into the travesty *Singspiel*-operettas of Offenbach. This French line is more many-sided, richer in variety than the Italian, but, on the other hand, even in its most important works not nearly so lasting. It is also striking that in the history of the French works their sociological background is clearly mirrored. From Rousseau, through Grétry, Boieldieu, Auber, and Adam, to Offenbach, it is the musical history of bourgeois society that is enacted.

In the Italian *buffa* it is harder to recognize such connections. It is of no consequence that Paisiello and Cimarosa wrote for the theatre of Catherine the Great in St. Petersburg, that Pergolesi wrote for Naples, and Rossini for Rome. The works themselves are greater in conception than those of the French, and all external sociological constituents are dissolved in pure music, leaving no trace. Such music was made possible by the *buffa* singer and his innate dramatic gifts.

La Serva padrona contains the distilled content of the whole species. Only two singing characters appear: a man and a woman. The third participant in the action is mute, serving as the ball that the others throw back and forth in play. Of the singers the woman is a mezzo-soprano, her part written not particularly high—at times rather low, in fact—and without coloratura. The man is a bass, likewise of medium range. Of both voices artistic skill is required, but no virtuoso singing technique. The style is that of speaking song throughout, directly so in the long recitatives. In the arias and duets it is compressed into concise flourishes, which expand into aria-melody through thematic development and periodic rounding out. One might call this short-breathed invention, put together almost out of mere motives, if its explanation did not lie rather in the very style of this musical speech, preserved by the declamation even in the shape of the vocal line.

Upon this natural, unforced relation—in which one cannot say which is primary, speech or song—rests the vitality of the work and its effectiveness on the stage. It is among the most astonishing things the theatre has to show in any age. Two speaking characters, no decoration—nothing could be more primitive. The play and counterplay of the sexes is made possible by this reduction to the utmost simplicity, because each sex is represented by its most characteristic feature: the voice, in undisguised sensuous appeal. Moreover, only this extreme simplification makes possible such total importance of the voice, such unhindered, naïve, direct vocal effect: the woman's inciting series of resistances and dissimulations, and the man's strength—clumsy at first, but finally asserting itself—which that slyly inflaming sex attraction calls forth.

The astonishing thing is the variety exhibited within that narrow circle. Nothing more can be said about the interplay of man and woman than bass and soprano tell each other and enact in their raving, dancing, and singing. It may be this element of eternal validity that gives Pergolesi's work its incomparable effect. Two great musical nations took this little work as the basis for what was to each of them one of its most important forms of creative activity; yet it remains, beyond all elaborations upon it, alive and inimitable. While it contained, as the first work, the essence of the entire species, it left to later times the possibility of formal expansion and productive elaboration. But everything essential it had itself established beyond excelling.

LA SERVA PADRONA is the theme. There follow the Italian and French variations.

They are variations from the artistic and pictorial

point of view as well as from the point of view of their form and content. Paisiello, Cimarosa, Rossini, Donizetti—as Italians, they form a single line. The theme of the high-born maiden (I speak of the inner sense, not of the subject matter) returns in each of them—at least in both versions of the BARBIERE and in DON PASQUALE. It broadly determines the tonal outline as well. This outline differentiates itself from Pergolesi's through the increased variety of characters. In this connection it is striking that only Cimarosa, in the MATRIMONIO SEGRETO, undertakes a three-fold division of the women's voices. Paisiello, Rossini, and Donizetti stick to one soprano, which they also limit to the lower middle range, though they give it an increasingly coloratura character. The song-bird quality, the quality that incites to love, becomes an end in itself. Woman in this art form is for the Italian merely a creature of sex, not a character.

The male characters show more gradations. Among them one gradually comes upon all the figures of the *commedia dell' arte,* transformed into appropriate vocal types and shaped with the ensemble in mind. Cimarosa has as his chief parts a tenor, a baritone, and a bass, with three corresponding women's parts, so that the resulting ensemble is the Mozart sextet. Paisiello adds to the three chief male parts, as Rossini does later, the deep character-bass of Basilio, and two tenors and two basses besides to fill out the ensemble. The second Finale, for him the most important, is a septet with one female voice.

Rossini gets along without the subsidiary parts. His big first finale is a sextet of two women's and four men's voices, with men's chorus. The latter was not customary in the *buffa*. Rossini inserted it in only two places: the Introduction and the first finale. In the former it is purely episodic; in the latter it contributes rhythmic and dynamic accentuation. But thorough exploitation of the full chorus for *buffo* effects was first undertaken by Donizetti in the most original number of his Don Pasquale—the chorus of servants. The group of soloists, on the other hand, he brings back to the simplicity of the quartet: soprano, tenor, lyric baritone, and *buffo*.

In this particular manner of distributing the voice-parts—that is, in the ensemble treatment of the voices —the development of the *buffa* from the foundation of the Serva padrona completes itself. The medium of intensification is the addition of the lyric tenor as lover. From his presence arises the dramatic and vocal character of the other figures, and thus the rounding out of the group into a musically mobile ensemble.

Development in the sense of growth from the standpoint of content is not to be found in the *buffa* series: each work represents an individual shade of essentially the same agreeable humor. The orchestral display remains modest: in Pergolesi there are only strings, and in the rest an orchestra of assorted instruments, confined to the function of accompaniment. Episodically there appear independent Intermezzi: in Paisiello and Rossini the storm music, with the favorite *crescendo* and *decrescendo* effects, and in Cimarosa the serenade-like night music. The structure is always two-part, with consequent emphasis upon the two final climaxes. These are particularly exploited by Cimarosa and Rossini, while Paisiello allows his first act to evaporate in the plaintive Cavatina of Rosina. It was through the addition of the Finale that Rossini achieved the success that caused Paisiello's hitherto universally beloved work to fall into oblivion. This was not alone the victory of genius pressing forward from bourgeois comedy into the sphere of pure *buffa*. It was at the same time the victory of the vocal ensemble over the opera of solo-singing.

Every soloist, to be sure, even in Rossini, has his aria. In these arias the characters are moulded by the voices. Figaro and Basilio especially take shape in the arias, the former by means of the virtuosity of his speaking ariosos, the latter through the diabolic depth of his vocal organ. The self-revelation of the hypocrite is so vividly developed in the contrast between thought and song, that Bartolo, who for the most part remains within *buffo* conventions, is almost suffocated by his partner. The tenor undergoes an intensification similar to that of the character-bass. He receives not alone the lyricism of the lover, but also the coloratura of the nightingale, the light, *parlando* agility of the *buffo,* and in the masquerade scenes the heroic accent of the soldier and the tone of the jesuitical fool.

But the widest range of expression is that of Figaro himself. Here is the man who has no need of a complementary woman's voice. He, like Basilio, the only worthy figure playing against him, is governed by the demon of gold. He could, again like Basilio, be a tragic figure, like his great vocal comrade, Don Giovanni. But his world is this side of tragedy. Thus he becomes the charioteer of fate, the go-between, the core of the ensemble. His voice, which leads, carries the middle line, on one side of which the *buffo* bass and the lyric tenor languish for a soprano, while on the other the merry philosopher-baritone and the Mephistophelian musician-bass become intoxicated with the idea of gold.

This is the situation of the Finale, which has no equal in the entire *buffa* literature. The voices, at first still singing and conscious of their own vocal lines, become more and more mere functional bearers of melodic, harmonic, and rhythmic accents. This solution is effected by the pace of the work, the nature of its construction and of its gradual building-up. It leads from the plane of the actual phenomena of the drama up into a sphere of unreal activity where only sounds, voices, rhythm, pursue one another in a ghostly chase. And here enter the deep tones of the chorus, making a completely deafening whole, achieving with their inexorable obstinacy the final climax in this world of tonal chaos.

This finale is, and must be according to the idea of the whole work, the peak of intensity. And it is so logically part and parcel of the whole that the earlier pieces lead in organic relation to it. The pieces that follow bring still another climax, but on the *buffo* rather than on the purely artistic side; especially the shaving quintet, which leads to ever madder boisterousness and ends in a dance-orgy of the voices. The second finale brings only the gay recapitulating backward glance and the conclusion, according to the requirements of artistic economy.

Rossini's BARBIERE, like Pergolesi's SERVA PADRONA, signifies the discovery of the greatest dramatic possibilities in voices. But what was only a ground-plan in the earlier work appears in its conclusive state in the later one. In both cases, the text is only a means of setting free the hidden energies of the voices. But in both cases the fundamental dramatic import, as well as the form taken by the text, stands in organic relation with the theatrical purpose of the singing. Thus there are here revealed, beyond the external and accidental nature of the libretto, fundamental relations between the spirit of the language and the tonal fabric. Out of these things arises that complete and self-contained art-work, the Italian *buffa*.

There are a large number of other Italian *buffo* operas—Rossini himself wrote several more. But since all were necessarily directed at the same goal, the outstanding work of the species has sent the others into oblivion. Only Donizetti's DON PASQUALE preserved, although at an appropriately modest distance, its own separate existence. Still, it is the last return of the SERVA PADRONA and represents, apart from the episode of the servants' chorus—a work of genius—a simplification of the lavish Rossini ensemble. Bearing the stamp of quartet-writing as it does, it stands as a style-conscious, slightly archaic, transitional, Biedermeier piece between the sextet-style of Rossini and the duet-style of Pergolesi. These three ensemble types describe the circle of the Italian *buffa*. In it a basic species of singing drama was realized, and a productive fusion of language and song achieved, corresponding entirely to the nature of the creative spirit of the people in all its purity.

2

The completely convention-free naturalism of the *buffa* had its effect in foreign countries as well, especially in France. For there seemed here a way of circumventing, or at least of diminishing the importance of, a lack in French vocal music. It had been demonstrated that the French singer, because of the hindrances offered by French sound-formations, could never approach the *bel canto* of the Italian, and would remain forever limited to rhetorical declamation. But if one simplified this melodic declamation, if one took from it all compulsion to seek the heights of pathos, if one limited it to simple, song-like singing of lyric episodes and connected these lyric passages with spoken dialogue, there arose a new and usable form. The things which had hitherto, because of the language, been weaknesses, were changed into merits. Musical naturalness was achieved.

Rousseau's LE DEVIN DU VILLAGE is the first French *Singspiel,* and it consciously leans on the Italian *buffa.* Evil tongues declared that the music was not by Rousseau, but no one has ever succeeded in producing proof of that allegation. The awkwardness of the realization makes his authorship credible. This little work, too, was a fanfare of the Return to Nature. The purpose was not only to express Nature in the sense of everyday people and events, but also to express the musical nature of a people as it becomes recognizable in that people's gift for song.

The French voice is at a natural disadvantage as compared not only with the Italian, but even with the German. It is flat, wavering (especially in women), and at the same time often shrill in quality. It receives, because of the nature of sound-formation in French, a painful, nasal resonance. It is unbeautiful simply taken as raw material, and its essential lack of beauty is aggravated by the unfavorable influence of the language. These prior handicaps make it unsuited to sustained song, while, on the other hand, all forms which are accented in rhythm and declamation suit it very well: the *chanson,* the couplet, in fact all those smaller, lyric forms which require tenderness of sentiment rather than lavish vocal resource.

Against the background of these conditions, the French *vaudeville,* directly occasioned by the visit of the Italian *buffo*-singers to Paris, was concocted in Rousseau's laboratory. It was artless, it was essentially popular. It avoided pretentious gestures and contented itself with simple singing. Thus it became a favorite form. Many talents tried their hand at it: Frenchmen like Philidor and Monsigny, and foreigners as well—the Italians Duni and Isouard, and the Belgian Grétry. French musical creation, particularly in the field of opera, numbers a higher percentage of foreigners in leading positions than is to be found in the achievement of any other people.

Out of the French *Singspiel,* the *opéra comique* grew. It is not to be considered the same as the German comic opera. In the *comique,* the lyric as well as the dramatic element is often more consciously emphasized than in the prevailing lighter German form. The *comique* boasts an immense series of works. Of them all, Boieldieu's LA DAME BLANCHE, Auber's FRA DIAVOLO, and Adam's LE POSTILLON DE LONJUMEAU still hold the boards. Some decades ago the *comique* ruled the theatres of Europe, which, to be sure, at that time took their lead entirely from Paris. Despite this forced distribution, despite the culture and the taste reflected in the best works, the *comique* never achieved the absolute world-significance that the *buffa* enjoyed from the moment of its birth. The *comique* was a form of practical significance, meeting practical needs, and it lacked the musical substance to become more than that. It was so frail because its mother-soil—French song—was so weak. Not singers, but makeshift singing-actors stood upon the stage. The situation was similar to that in Germany, but with this important difference: that in Germany the undeveloped state of the art of singing and the hindrances offered by the language were gradually circumvented, whereas in France such circumvention was, owing to the nature of the talents and the language, more difficult.

Thus the protagonist of the *comique* remained the singing-actor. Its most characteristic type is the exceptionally high-ranged, light, agile, coloratura-type lyric tenor. He appears as the romantic gallant, the heartbreaker, once openly, as in George Brown, another time disguised as a knave, as in FRA DIAVOLO, and again changed from peasant to fine gentleman, as in the POSTILLON. He is always a sort of salon-ized, tenor-ized Don Giovanni, seducing the women and deceiving the men. His partner is the French soubrette, coquettish yet genuinely emotional. She sings songs, ballades, romanzas, and decks them out with bravura coloratura passages, without attempting the great Italian coloratura style.

These two are the chief figures of the *comique*. Occasionally the soubrette takes on a lyric character, or, as in LA DAME BLANCHE, another rôle, a really singing part is added. Or, as in FRA DIAVOLO, the tenor part is doubled, and to the rakish *bon vivant* is added the lyric rôle of a lover. All the other rôles perform dramatic functions—above all the two bandits, the tenor *buffo* and the bass *buffo,* the bass as father, uncle, villain. All are dramatic types made to sing in a manner appropriate to their significance in the drama. Hence the ever-recurring forms of the drinking song, with and without chorus, the prayer, the hunting-song, the romanza, the barcarole, the cradle- or slumber-song, the song of reminiscence, and similar forms. They are inserted as lyric, musical points of repose, but are so thoroughly worked in from the dramatic point of view that there arises a free and natural connection between dramatic realism and song.

Thence follows the necessity of continually finding new texts. As long as the emphasis was upon song as such, the repeated recurrence of the same words made no difference. But the more the texts aim at close connection of dramatic and vocal effect, the greater becomes the unceasing demand for new texts. Once a scaffolding for the composer, around which to build his music, the text now becomes a continually changing costume, clothing a fundamentally unchanging music. Novels, short stories, anecdotes, episodes, present an excuse, in their ever new arrangements of external events, for decking out bare song-forms in the appearance of novelty.

There are several scenic climaxes arranged with particular cleverness: the auction in the second act of La Dame blanche, the nocturnal invasion in Fra Diavolo, the abduction of Chappelou in the first act of Le Postillon. In each case it is in the focal finale of the work that all the threads are drawn together. Through apparent confusion of the dramatic forces, clever use of the chorus, well-arranged dynamic climaxes in the orchestra as well, the impression of dramatic intensification is created. And in contrast to *opera buffa,* the chorus is especially active as an inciting factor, just as it is in German opera.

Despite these often original individual traits, *opéra comique* does not exceed the significance of a hybrid species. Its vital force consists entirely in the entertaining character of its subject matter, and the musical, singing *buffa* in the Italian sense remains a closed book to it. No one succeeded in loosening the connection of the *comique* with dramatic elements sufficiently for music and song to take the lead. It has not enough singers, or enough variety among the singers it has. It is smothered in dialogue, and does not permit its musical forms to expand. This lack is not made up for by the cleverness of inventive text writers, or by the giftedness of composers, or by the external success of a genre which is ingratiating and satisfies a weary time's need for rest.

The way indicated by Jean Jacques Rousseau had shown this *genre* to be available, and had opened many attractive vistas. But it was not a highway, nor did it suggest the possibility of further development, or indeed of the setting of any goal. It ended in the blind alley of Adam's artificial *Singspiel*. From this point on, only the miniature form of the lyric one-act work, or the operetta, was possible. Both reached their conclusion in Offenbach's romantic irony.

The *buffa,* too, had fulfilled its possibilities. It could repeat itself but it could achieve no further intensification. Out of the feeling of fulfilment there comes a time of pleasant satiety, at least in the Romance countries—that is, outside Germany. Mozart was not contemporary. His music was respected and admired, but his operas were without any relation to his day. FIDELIO had little influence, and of the domestic German movement introduced by DER FREISCHÜTZ other countries of artistic importance were hardly conscious. Vienna, to be sure, boasted an excellent opera-house, but no artistic events of any significance had occurred there in years. In Milan the serious work of the young Sicilian, Bellini—the tragic opera NORMA—had excited attention. Constructed in simple forms, as in Gluck's imitation of the antique, it did not exceed the trio, as far as ensembles went; it relegated the chorus once more to the position of accessory; and it concentrated all its force on the characterization of the title-rôle, which was treated as that of a coloratura heroine with a solid basis in *cantabile* singing. With similar earnestness and amiable solemnity, Méhul tried his hand at the almost oratorio-like JOSEPH. This opera owes its peculiar tone-coloring to the fact that, with the exception of the rôle of Benjamin, sung by a woman, only men's voices are used in it.

In Paris two men of greater originality had come to the fore, two gallicized Italians—Cherubini and Spontini. Cherubini, descended from the *buffa,* had established in LODOÏSKA, FANISKA, and THE WATER-CARRIERS, the bourgeois tragic opera of the Revolution,

WEBER
Born at Eutin in Holstein 1786.
died in London Monday June the 5th 1826.
Drawn and executed in lithography by Minasi (Artist to the King of Naples &c)
and most respectfully dedicated by him with their permission to the directors and subscribers of
the Philharmonic Society
Pale genius strives in vain to check a sigh,
And points in silence to his laurell'd bust:
While all the tuneful nine sit drooping by.
Nor does Britannia, generous maid, Forget
What to this unassuming worth is due;
But marks with sympathy and deep regret,
The cheerless scene which opens to her view,
Observes with plaintive eye where he is laid
And drops a tear of pity to his shade.

which found its fulfilment in FIDELIO. Beside him and following him appeared Spontini, likewise descended from the *buffa,* but later suddenly adopting the apparatus of the large-scale, heroic opera. Thus the Italians were again everywhere in the van, but, significantly, with a strong leaning towards Paris and its grand opera.

There everything was to be found which the composer needed for opera: the stage with its mechanical magic-apparatus, decoration, costumes, the great orchestra, countless personnel, and in addition the festive brilliance before and behind the footlights, powerful, heroic emotions, tragic conflicts, choruses, ballets. Into this reservoir of theatrical art all the forces of opera production, which had been growing in every separate field since Mozart's day, could empty themselves as soon as one basic demand had been satisfied: the demand for Nature and naturalism.

But how had such a demand become applicable to opera? Was it not descended from that spirit of enlightenment, current in the 18th century, which had already, as a philosophic outlook, been superseded and fallen into disrepute? What had this demand accomplished in connection with the opera? Apart from the unique case of the Italian *buffa,* which was also no longer productive, it had effected only the general stagnation of all forces, the débacle of production directed at high aims, the preference for purely entertaining diminutive genres.

It had repressed both the art and the personality of the great singer. What had become of the productive pursuit of the art of singing? The creative musician had laid aside his noblest medium of characterization. He had turned his attention to the orchestra or to reflection about naturalism in song and declamation. The difficulties of the language-problem had captured him, and dramaturgic technique and the problems of artistic reasoning now seemed more important than anything concerning singers and voices.

Was it right to travel further along this road?

Now a great reaction set in. The much-celebrated naturalism of the opera turned into its opposite. A great love broke forth again for the most beautiful medium of dramatic expression—the singing voice. Once the voice had been both object and subject of the drama, giving it its impetus. Now it again became the chief factor, so irresistible that it forced all the other elements into its service, and became an end in itself.

But a great enervation came over men. They recognized in the sensuous no longer spiritual forces, but only exterior appeal. There arose the joy of playing with this appeal: the impulse to virtuosity. There appeared the archetype of the virtuoso, the demon Paganini, and, called forth by and emulating him, his counterpart,

Franz Liszt. There appeared singers of more than passing importance—among them the Pasta, the Malibran, Jenny Lind, Rubini, Lablache, etc. There appeared the great virtuoso of the orchestra, Hector Berlioz. There occurred the conjunction of all the virtuoso arts of the stage in the magic of stage illusion. But all were led by the chief representative of this new (and at the same time ancient) art of most intense artistic ecstasy: the virtuoso singer.

He stands no longer alone, however, but side by side with every conceivable type, in the virtuoso ensemble led by the virtuoso composer. They all herald the power of the singing voice in characterization. This power now shows itself in the externally most sumptuous of the metamorphoses it has yet undergone: that of virtuosity become an end in itself in opera.

Chapter VII

OPÉRA

THE city of the *opéra* is Paris, but its creators are more often Italians and Germans than Frenchmen. The founder is an Italian, Lully; later comes the German, Gluck; there follow the Italians, Spontini and Rossini, and finally the German, Meyerbeer. In between there stand the Frenchmen—Rameau, Méhul, Halévy, Auber. But apart from Rameau, none of them is the equal of the foreigners, and none is in any way favored. The large proportion of foreigners among the leading musicians of the great *Institut,* against which nobody protested, shows that the French looked upon this organization as a union of all forces streaming into the cosmopolis, as proof of a cosmopolitan art under the French banner. Like the *seria* in Italy, the Opéra in Paris was open to musicians of all nationalities, as long as they composed to texts in the French language.

The democratic idea of the Revolution confirmed this

tendency towards musical internationalism, and composers of all countries responded to it. For in Paris were the richest and most highly developed means of every sort, the most favorable conditions for production. Among these was the most widely influential and intellectually most active press.

It was not only the cultural atmosphere that favored freedom from prejudice in matters of nationality. Opéra itself bore the mark of an international hybrid art. The typically French elements in grand opera had never been song, but rather declamatory recitative and the ballet.

The ballet led grand opera into a form-world unlike anything known elsewhere. The influence hereby implied was not limited to the interpolation of a few dance movements. The ballet as an element of illustration determined the mimetic style of the sung portions as well. Moreover, the inner, organic structure—and so finally the aesthetic essence—of French opera as a species was decisively influenced by it. This opera is a mythological allegory, not only in its subject matter but in its inner spirit as well. While Italian opera is born of song, French grand opera is born of the dance, of the art of form through movement. In French opera, song at first serves as a declamatory connection between the dances; mute pantomime then dissolves in rhetoric, and only finally does the stylized lyricism of the melodic aria appear.

This was the weak point of French music, and thus of the *opéra* as well. Because of its origin in the language of the body, the *opéra* bore within itself every possibility of expanding into a medium of expression of great force. Because of its declamatory possibilities it was fitted for high pathos, and thus for the genuine tragic style. But its melodic barrenness and vocal poverty made it eagerly accept every musically enriching force, no matter of what origin. Only when enhanced by this alien power of melodic song could the forces locked up in the basic impulse of the dance properly unfold. With the utmost variety of means of illustration, from mere use of the body to most lavish development of scenic and costume effects, these forces grew into a veritable apotheosis of dance and song.

French opera is certainly more than a mere apotheosis of the dance. But in the musically stylized movement of the body the unreality of opera found a new means of expression. The tendency of the *opéra* is always to achieve a dramatic union of the melodic element of song with the rhythmic element of the dance. The dramatic factor is not to be understood in relation only to the human body. It embraces in the widest sense everything visual, every optical effect.

Thus grand opera is essentially a compilatory form,

not in the sense of a mere external collection of things which are by nature incompatible, but in the will to create a super-organism. It is lured on by an art-dream of high aspiration. The ideal of a new world-citizenship is dawning, which, grounded in middle-class democracy, and working according to the principles of a reasonable equalizing of forces, aims to give form in an art of imposing proportions to a universal creation. It wants to enjoy the fruits of all previous achievements. It is, that is to say, a movement of aspiration, whose creative characteristic is the desire for comprehensiveness in the widest measure.

This desire had always been implicit in the nature of the *opéra,* but it could not always and with constant energy be explicitly effective. When the *Institut* was founded, in 1669, Venetian opera was in full flower, Neapolitan opera was coming into existence, and in Hamburg the effort was being made to create a German opera. This period was the less favorable to the idea of comprehensiveness since the *opéra* at that time was purely an entertainment for the court. The first German invasion, by Gluck, led to lively literary exchanges without robbing the species of the flavor of a non-popular, court art; it remained far from actual life. It was in Spontini's works that a change in the direction of actuality, and thus towards a broadening of its effect, first took place. Opera now treated historical subjects with clear reference to contemporary events. La Vestale, produced in 1807, introduces analogy with the Roman world of triumphal processions and martial sounds, hitherto neglected in the opera. Ferdinand Cortez, given in 1809, Spontini's most important and far-reaching success, is the glorification of the conqueror. Olympia, first produced in 1819 after Napoleon's fall, likewise reflects the history of the period in that, following Voltaire, it treats a subject from the time of the Diadochi. These works are forgotten, for Spontini was not musically long-breathed enough to keep them alive as stage-works after their immediate actuality had passed. But they point the new path of grand opera: the desire for representative, universal application, over and above individual artistic problems. The means of achieving that goal is the actuality of the subject chosen.

In the works that follow, by Auber, Rossini, Meyerbeer, with their basis in revolutionary, political, religious, and sociological ideas, actuality is intensified until it becomes unqualified up-to-dateness. If ever there was a timely opera which attempted to bring the musical theatre into the very center of life by connecting it with the ideas of the day, it was the grand opera of the pre-1848 period. It was a political theatre of the times on the grandest scale, or at least this was what it aimed to be. All the inciting ideas of those years were given the broadest utterance through the example of some important historical parallel.

From this arose the need for monumentality in external arrangements. Out of the original three acts four or five were made, each of hitherto unusual length. The subject grows luxuriantly, beyond restraint; massiveness becomes an aesthetic necessity.

This urge towards expansion affects the voices also. Their range is stretched both upward and downward. They are forced to combine power and lyric quality. The demands made upon their purely physical possibilities exceed anything known before. Since few singers meet these requirements, it becomes customary in actual practice to simplify and abbreviate the parts. The composer's indications represent only an ideal on paper from which each singer strikes out the parts that do not suit him. The musical text is at the mercy of the singer's caprice, just as it once had been in Italian opera, only with opposite effect: then the singer used to elaborate upon his texts; now he simplifies them.

Thus the composer builds up his own ideal of the virtuoso singer, taking instrumental virtuosity as his model. The nature of the melodic construction, too, is determined from an instrumental point of view, and regard for words and text plays no rôle at all. Since the purport of the plot is told in the recitative, language is a side-issue in the arias.

The very treatment of the voices gives evidence of the same desire for superhuman dimensions. All the extreme registers are preferred. Basses cannot go low enough, tenors and sopranos cannot go high enough. The strangely unrealistic tone of the female contralto, never made use of in opera before, is adopted for dominating characters. The coloratura soprano, displayed in passages of the most daring instrumental character, appears in two guises: as a singer of dramatic force, and as a soubrette playing the character of a page. The coloratura tenor, too, reappears, wherever possible as a prince, and the coloratura soprano as a princess. On the other hand, the most important male voice, the baritone, plays in the course of later development a rôle just as subsidiary as that of the dramatic mezzo-soprano. Only Rossini's GUILLAUME TELL is an exception. This work already shows all the marks of the new mammoth style, yet remains within the limits of artistic reality.

The ensemble of singing forces, viewed as a whole, shows the generation of baroque heroic voices in the ascendant, as seen from the Italian side. Vocal power, fullness, and endurance, always combined with good voice culture and an impressive physical appearance, are prerequisites. These are heroes by virtue of external magnification only, it is true. Their behavior is passive, and their effect is limited to the physical impressiveness of their voices.

Thus grand opera is an enlargement in every respect. The forced breadth of view is intended to give the impression of monumentality. This opera aims to be heroic in every way. It takes its concept of the heroic from the great two-dimensional mural paintings that were being produced during the same period. And it shares with these paintings the symbolic application of historic subjects to contemporary events.

Thus grand opera is an ensemble art of a peculiar nature. It is ensemble in the sense not of unification, but of superimposed joining of parts. What it lacks in organic unity, it makes up for in the sovereign strategy of the combined effect. The chorus achieves significance as a mass. Just as in German romantic opera, but more consciously, the people become an element in the plot, which concerns itself with the soul of the masses in relation to revolutionary, religious, or sociological ideas. Out of this subsoil grow the big ensembles. They constitute the artistic kernel of grand opera and find their culmination in the finale. In them nothing survives of the feeling for the individual and for naturalness that pervaded Mozart's finales. The ballet-like, symmetrical movement of the voices as well, as exemplified in the finale of Rossini's BARBER, lies in the far distance. The singing voice in grand opera is not a person or a soul. It is a virtuoso tone-product of ever-changing color, supported by the many times subdivided chorus, complemented by the solo ensemble, which is arranged in several groups that share in the execution.

The whole rests upon the orchestra, capable of every dynamic climax and ever competing with the voices. The entire ensemble is architectonically constructed. The building materials are simple, plastically impressive, instrumental themes which unfold in widely extended harmonic expansion. The individuality of single details vanishes: the whole becomes an all-embracing harmonic unity of tone-colors.

Into this ensemble, apparently only as an external interruption, but actually as an inner and determining factor, comes the ballet. It creates, in the first place, a contrast in the course of the vocal development, out of which the voices then rise again with heightened effect. Thus the form of the whole is really determined by the dance. The ballet is based upon the closed dance form as it occurs in the ball-room dances of the period, especially in the walking dances: the *contredanse* and *quadrille*. And, working backwards, these dances are then taken out of the opera and adopted again for ball-room use.

Here the strong connection of all the figures with the basic law of rhythmic movement is evident. They are never, they cannot and are not intended to be, human beings. They are figures moving in the dance. Out of dance movement they develop the nature of their singing and the form of their song. Complete agreement of appearance, dance movement, and song is the end sought. Out of this idea of the movement and counter-movement of groups, the juxtaposition of slower and faster moving sections, grows the structure of the ensembles and finales. It mirrors an idea of form essentially derived from bodily movement. This idea is then converted into what might be called optical music, into a great dance—now solemn, now unrestrained, now tender—of all the singing and resounding voices.

The allegory of old French opera reappears in a new incarnation. The subject matter in which it is now clothed is historical, but the intellectual content is contemporary. Moreover, there is a greater fullness of performing forces, as regards the vocal, instrumental, and scenic resources and the mobilization of all intellectual factors. But over and above all these details, the foundation remains the same: the ballet with connecting recitatives. This ballet is now danced, now sung. As far as stylistic significance is concerned, the scope of the sung and danced portions is the same. Ballet can be a sort of pantomime on a foundation of dancing; it can, with singing and words, be developed into scenic and choreographic drama. Thus grand opera combines all possibilities within the frame of singing action. It is not without hidden significance that in the first work of the species, by Auber, the title rôle is a mute character and is portrayed by a dancer.

More important than this single though symptomatic case is recognition of the fact that the whole grand opera species is basically determined by dance gesture, by the creative impulse of bodily movement. Thus grand opera appears as the highest achievement possible to combined song, language, and gesture, with bodily movement as the leading factor, just as *opéra comique* is the result of a combination in which language has the leading function.

The grand opera of the 19th century is, in accordance with its eclectic, compilatory nature, a species in a larger sense than the *buffa*. Essentially, its historical as well as its aesthetic nature is almost independent of the personalities of its composers. The sociological character predominates, and from the specifically artistic point of view individual works are distinguished from one another only to the extent to which they fulfill the conditions of the species. After Spontini's preparatory work, pointing the way, there follows about 1830 a sudden volcanic eruption: LA MUETTE DE PORTICI of Auber in 1829; Rossini's TELL in 1830; and again a year later, in 1831, Meyerbeer's ROBERT LE DIABLE. From this point on Meyerbeer becomes the leading figure. He is the concluding representative of grand opera.

This distinction belongs to Meyerbeer only as judged by successes. Meyerbeer had not the temperamental buoyancy of Auber, who made the MUETTE into a real work of revolution. Still less had he the inventive genius of Rossini, who nevertheless, like Auber, did not achieve more than one complete concentration of forces. He had unusual judgment, cultured taste, and great powers of industry. He was the genius of virtuosity in composition. As such he rounded out and perfected in all directions the matured grand opera species. Besides ROBERT, he wrote three important works: LES HUGUENOTS, 1836; LE PROPHÈTE, 1848; and L'AFRICAINE, first performed after his death, in 1865. Supplementary to these works of Meyerbeer are Halévy's LA JUIVE, which appeared in 1835, and—harbinger of a coming time—the coarsened, German version of the Paris opera-type: Wagner's RIENZI, 1842. That ends the series which makes up the species known as "grand opera."

Characteristic of Meyerbeer as distinguished from his predecessors, and bearing witness to his German origin, is his treatment of the orchestra. Upon it rests the construction of the organism as a whole. The orchestra, so to speak, receives a charter of its own, and is placed at a critical distance from the stage. Virtuosos appear within it and compete in concert style with the virtuosos on the stage. New elements are the sumptuousness of the color-blending, especially among the woodwinds, and the original effects and rhythmic vigor among the instruments of percussion. The exciting effect of these works is due not least to their sensuous, ingratiating orchestral tone. Meyerbeer is particularly fond of keys with many accidentals in the signature, doubtless because of the unusual tonal appeal of the soft woodwinds in these keys.

From the character of the orchestral tone there follows corresponding expansion of the vocal mass, of solo effects, and of the general architecture of the work. The length of the road Meyerbeer had put behind him is shown by a comparison of the Benediction of the Swords in LES HUGUENOTS with its earlier prototype: the Rütli oath in Rossini's GUILLAUME TELL. Although the force of Rossini's form is still directly effective, yet it seems as if Meyerbeer really only begins where Rossini leaves off. To be sure, Rossini's form would not have been capable of organic expansion. But in Meyerbeer there existed the possibility of realizing a much broader conception, as a result of the organization of the orchestra with that end in view. Rossini ends with the climax; Meyerbeer steers with extreme virtuosity back into the *decrescendo,* and achieves by so doing his great buoyancy of line.

It pleased the time that followed Meyerbeer to plunder his art and then to make him the scapegoat for the aesthetic hybridism of grand opera. Now, Meyerbeer did not invent grand opera; he developed it along the lines possible to him. It is true that this development was a matter of sheer talent and took place without much critical judgment in the higher sense. With all his great gifts, Meyerbeer found no way to give to the many-sidedness of the *opéra* a creative focus.

The question suggests itself whether any attention would have been paid to an attempt to do so. The fate of Berlioz's BENVENUTO CELLINI (which dates from 1838) is an example. Here Berlioz adapted the means of grand opera to an artistic drama, and wrote a great deal of beautiful music for it. But this music for the most part lacks directness of theatrical effect. It is a great symphonic work with scenic illustrations. A single scene, constructed on a grandiose scale—the Roman Carnival—really achieves the color and form of the theatre through its elementary connection with the dance. And Berlioz is an even greater stranger to the human voice than Beethoven. CELLINI remains a symphonic fantasy, and its closer adaptation to opera form does not really bring it any nearer to the theatre than LA DAMNATION DE FAUST or ROMÉO ET JULIETTE. Showing conceptions of genius in all scenes of a dance character, especially in the *buffo* trio in the first act, CELLINI remains, even in important climaxes in the plot and especially in the dramatically decisive scene of the casting of the Perseus statue, dry and lifeless.

Comparison with Cellini shows the superiority of Meyerbeer's style. A glance at the serious and in individual details almost holy beauties of La Juive, again, shows that Halévy possessed a considerably more versatile musical personality. But even Halévy could not overcome the unorganically heterogeneous nature of the elements that flow together to make grand opera. It is true that Eléazar, the paternal heroic tenor, whose racial character is portrayed with special originality through the choice of registers, is a vocal type new to the operatic stage; that the lyric-dramatic Rachel and the bass rôle of the Cardinal bear the stamp of genuine and realistic humanity; and that vocal ensembles, like those in the Passover celebration in the second act and the *a cappella* choruses in the execution scene, show the hand of a master very happily inspired by his inner ear for vocal effects.

But despite these beauties, which are distributed throughout the entire opera, La Juive remains an isolated example. It changes not at all the nature of the *opéra* as a representational art in the great style. Subjects of contemporary interest, in historical disguise, take the place of the myth upon which the old ballet-opera was based, set to music by the master-virtuoso, sung, danced, and played by virtuosos of the stage, and given pictorial form by virtuoso mechanical means. The audience of grand opera is the society of all the nations of Europe. This society gives grand opera its social frame. Indeed it does more than that: it actually represents the reflection in real life of the unreality on the stage.

Grand opera is really not an art-work in the usual sense. It is the creation of an entire community and an entire period, and as such it cannot be treated from the point of view of aesthetic criticism. It is in fact the first appearance of a sort of collectivist art species. Thus it is possible for now one and now another of its special attributes to stand out without affecting the whole, for this whole is not, and is not intended to be, a deeply-rooted organism.

Because of this fact, grand opera offers to parody a broad field of attack, and witty travesty grows to the importance of a complementary phenomenon. Thus Offenbach belongs to the history of grand opera as much as Meyerbeer. Offenbach does not make fun of Meyerbeer the musician, fond as he is of using Meyerbeer's pompous rhythms. Nor does he make fun of Rossini the musician, although GUILLAUME TELL returns in Offenbach's BELLE HÉLÈNE; nor of Gluck, although the lament of Orpheus achieved greater popularity through Offenbach's quotation of it than it did in Gluck's original version. But these individual references are only incidental. What Offenbach makes fun of is grand opera as such, the façade-monumentality of its forms, the falseness of its emotional speech derived from the stylization of the dance, its questionable virtuosity, the senselessness of its texts.

There exists no sharper criticism of grand opera than that in the great parodies of Offenbach, and none more just. This is the self-criticism of the period, making fun of its own work. It knows its own weaknesses best and sees the wrong side as clearly as the right. For this reason, there are to be found as few parallels to Offenbach's parodies as to grand opera. One must go back to the late period of Greek tragedy, where similar manifestations occurred in the plays of Euripides and Aristophanes.

Yet grand opera was a success. It made the places where it was performed in Paris the leading musical stages of the world. All other European theatres only followed in their wake. This domination had a paralyzing effect, much more general than that which Italian opera had exerted. The latter remained confined to the leading social circles of the time, and preserved its character by holding fast to the original language. But grand opera encountered a changed world. Theatres which were still nominally conducted as court theatres had long been open to the public and had become, although a part of the court establishment, the theatre of the middle class. The press, which in the 18th century had confined itself chiefly to special aesthetic considerations, had now introduced new modes of popular discussion and evaluation. But in the main it discussed only the individual artistic achievements of the time, not an art-form as such, since for this the needed perspectives hardly existed.

Robert Schumann concentrated his rage against LE PROPHÈTE in a diary-entry, but that secret gesture meant nothing as against the reports, influenced by Parisian opinion, that appeared in all German newspapers, or the wide distribution made possible by a growing music-business in the form of arrangements of favorite melodies, fantasies, and potpourris. The non-vocal nature of the opera, its acceptance as music that might be just as well whistled or played on a fiddle or a flute, was confirmed in every way. Thus the opera came to appear as an art-form in which favorite melodies were performed by favorite singers with the added attraction of effective staging and historical costumes. Scenes of bathing, skating, shooting, explosion, massacre, shipwreck, and other picturesque catastrophes, provided the necessary treats for the eye, yielding nothing to the circus. RIENZI sums up this sort of finale-climax, and the fracas in DIE MEISTERSINGER looks back humorously upon it.

Worst of all was the fact that foreign opera had to be sung on German stages in translation. And translation not only disturbed the relationship between tone and speech. Their barbaric lack of consideration for enunciation set the language of the German stage back into a state which had seemed outgrown a century ago. In addition, the sense of the original text, where the words made any sense at all, was often changed into its exact opposite for the sake of a rhyme or a turn of phrase.

But it was in this manner that the practical triumph of grand opera was achieved. It found its confirmation in the fact that Meyerbeer, like Spontini before him, was now called as *Generalmusikdirektor* to Berlin. He divided his activity as artistic director between Berlin and Paris. In Vienna, Munich, and Dresden, other advocates of grand opera exercised the directorial authority. The situation was not so bad in Italy, which still had the inexhaustible treasure of its native song-opera to set against the influence of the Parisian stage. Besides, the Italian public was less in need of renewal, and less lacking in leaders, than the German middle class. Nevertheless Italy, too, felt the influence of grand opera and the related problems of integrating extra-vocal elements into the entity of scenic vocal play. In Italy, as well as in Germany, there was eagerness for a settlement with this strange phenomenon which had overpowered all the forces of the lyric theatre.

OPÉRA

The settlement came. It brought with it the greatest creative renewal that is to be found in the history of opera since Mozart. It leads back from cosmopolitan to national opera, and is connected with the names of Wagner and Verdi.

Chapter VIII

WAGNER

I

THE time had come. Instinctively, and yet as if following a preconceived plan, several generations had prepared the way for one man to follow.

With the decline of Italian song-opera the operatic organism had burst its shell. Language had sprung it open. Song, plot, stage setting, representation, dialogue, recitative, aria, had become thoroughly confused, especially outside Italy. Gradually, to be sure, things seemed to have straightened themselves out again. Opera, built up of dance, song, and tableau, the great masquerade of the voices, existed in a new form. It seemed an exhibition of the most varied possibilities, waiting for one who should take from them all that which could again produce a genuine organism. And he came and took everything: Weber, Marschner, Lortzing, Spontini, Rossini, Auber, Halévy, Meyerbeer.

WAGNER

A few dates are important, because they are usually misconceived. Rienzi was written from 1839 to 1841 and shows the influence of Spontini's Ferdinand Cortez, and only to a lesser extent of Meyerbeer, with whose Les Huguenots Wagner became acquainted only while he was at work on Rienzi. Le Prophète appeared in 1848, several years after Der fliegende Holländer and Tannhäuser. When L'Africaine was first performed, in 1865, after Meyerbeer's death, Wagner was already occupied with Die Meistersinger. The dates of Wagner's works, then, parallel and do not follow Meyerbeer's. Meyerbeer achieved his apparent headstart through the rapid spread of his works. This headstart was so great that it made Meyerbeer, only twenty-two years older than Wagner, and moreover a very deliberate worker, seem almost to belong to an earlier age.

All the more striking is the definiteness and speed with which Wagner in his first works—Die Feen, Das Liebesverbot, and Rienzi—gathered together and critically reviewed all the elements of German, Italian, and French opera. These early works have not, to be sure, held their place on the stage, except for occasional performances of Rienzi—mostly in distorted form. But they lay the basis for Wagner's attitude towards opera. The compositions as well as what he wrote about them bear witness to the fact that Wagner was concerned, from the very beginning of his writing, with song—with singing beings on the stage. "Now, song is the one medium," he writes at the age of twenty-one, "through which a man can express himself musically, and if it is not perfectly developed he lacks his true speech. In this respect the Italians have an immense advantage over us, for with them beauty in song is second nature, and their voices, too, are as warm sensuously as they are lacking, from other points of view, in individual character . . . and yet I shall never forget the impression that a Bellini opera only recently made upon me, when I was thoroughly satiated with the eternal symbolic tumult of the orchestra, and once again encountered the noble simplicity of song."

The Bellini opera in question was I CAPULETTI ED I MONTECCHI. Wilhelmine Schröder-Devrient sang Romeo. Her magnificent achievement brought recognition of a second fact: that song must not be an end in itself, but must grow out of some inner relation with an essentially dramatic purpose. The person who taught that lesson through her singing was a woman. Thus Wagner had received decisive inspiration for vocal characterization: the living prototype of the female dramatic singing voice, and the construction of all singing organisms around that voice as a center.

Until that time German opera had, for dramatic female parts, contented itself with makeshifts. Leonore was to too great an extent a singing *idea* to have the effect of a woman with all the human limitations of woman. This is true not only of her dramatic significance, but also of her singing, and of the way in which the female voice is inserted in FIDELIO. The women in Weber's and Marschner's works are simply voice parts written in the treble clef, and not—with the exception of the bravura part of Rezia—living human beings. It is with Wagner that important rôles for the dramatic female voice begin. While he makes it the center of the singing action, after the pattern of Schröder-Devrient, he simultaneously establishes the basis upon which the new unity of opera is founded.

The female voice is better adapted than the male to dramatic effect, more flexible, and because of its pitch better suited to virtuoso treatment. So far as the old opera laid stress upon proportion and dramatic effect, it had been to the exclusion of any expression of feminine eroticism. Mozart had liberated the emotional power of the female voice. But leadership remained with the male voice, so that the female voice, even over and above its special abilities, was driven to the use of decoration and of the attractions of singing as an art.

As the female voice takes over the dramatic emphasis and becomes the leading part in the ensemble, all expressive formulae of virtuoso origin fall away. The voice takes on form and interest through the acute attraction between it and the voice of its partner. Female and male voices are conceived as divisions of an original whole whose halves are ever striving towards reunion. This urge, resting upon the need for complementary voices, gives them their dramatic significance. The attraction of the sexes becomes the object of the vocal plot. It is the part of the female voice to sound the calls of allurement and promise and of the male voice to express the search for fulfilment.

Thus the female voice becomes the dramatically activating factor. Weber, in the figures of Eglantine and Rezia, and Meyerbeer in Valentine, and later in Fides and Selica, had attempted something similar, but both without realizing the central significance of the road which they had opened. Wagner, realizing with ever-increasing penetration the vocal characterization of woman dominated by her longing for man, achieves for his drama not only its inner driving force but also the male vocal types that group themselves around this female voice in greatest possible variety.

Wagner's female voices do not exhibit the variety of Mozart's. There are in Wagner, as a matter of fact, only two different female characters. They are twin characters, complementing each other, forming an antithesis. It is true that he did not always make use of the dual female characters: Senta remains alone; Isolde, too, in comparison with whom Brangäne seems subordinate, as does Lene in comparison with Eva; while the tonal complement to Kundry is taken care of by the group of flower-maidens. But Venus and Elisabeth, Elsa and Ortrud, Brünnhilde and Sieglinde, are twin characters. Essentially belonging together, they radiate their conceptual relationship in two opposite directions. This is Wagner's later method of characterization. In RIENZI, the full-blown dramatic female voice still appears in the character of a man. Adriano is the aftermath of the Romeo of Schröder-Devrient, for whom the part was written—a dramatic mezzo-soprano, not an alto. This, too, is proof of the primary significance of the vocal characterization and the only secondary importance of the plot, which is external. The dramatic female voice as such was more important to Wagner than the scenic unreality of the heroic rôle sung by a woman in man's clothing—a contradiction such as he later avoided.

In comparison with the female voices hitherto used, Wagner's selection shows an abrupt curtailment. All the soubrette voices disappear, the TANNHÄUSER shepherd being the one relic of that species. The Rhine-maidens, the Norns, and the Valkyries are a new species of female ensemble, foreshadowed by the ensemble of the three women's voices in the ZAUBERFLÖTE. Within the individual works they serve as a sort of substitute for the chorus, to which the flower girls are a direct transition. From Lortzing, with whom he still maintains manifold relations, Wagner takes over the comic alto in MEISTERSINGER, while the HOLLÄNDER Mary he takes from the French play-opera. Apart from the figures already mentioned, the female voice appears only episodically: as Fricka and Waltraute and, in an impressive exploitation of the contralto tone, as Erda, the deep and heavy register being interpolated here as the high and agile register is for the forest bird. These details are exceptions with special purposes. They confirm their own distinction from the basic female voice types of the main plot: the single dramatic soprano, or the twin figures of the lyric soprano and the dramatic mezzo.

In both figures Wagner sees woman; or rather, he hears woman, the song of woman calling to man. Everything else is subsidiary: this is the kernel. In Senta's ballad the whole concept of Wagner's tonal dramaturgy is stated. But now this one voice is divided, not merely for the sake of dramatic fancy but as a matter of vocal technique and vocal economics. To combine the maiden and the woman in a single figure is to stretch too far the actual possibilities of the voice. Schröder-Devrient herself was not a success as Senta. So Wagner returns to the RIENZI division, except that the really dramatic female voice now belongs, in physical appearance as well, to a woman. The sublime and mighty voice of Schröder-Devrient becomes Venus, and the counter-figure—modeled after Wagner's young niece Johanna—more tender, less passionate, becomes Elisabeth.

The saint and the goddess of sinful love are not sharply contrasted; occasionally the two parts are even sung by the same singer. This situation confirms the inner identity of the two figures. Elisabeth, particularly, has more of the Venus element in her than, from the standpoint of the third act, she is credited with. One might think there had been a cleft in the conception, followed by a forced change in the character—above all in its vocal behavior, which changes only in the third act from the impulsive and the dramatic to the pure lyric.

Elisabeth and Venus never meet. Elsa and Ortrud are in actual conflict with each other: the vocal and dramatic situation is different, but the effect remains doubtful. Out of the direct juxtaposition of the two female voices arises the loosely organized character of the second act of Lohengrin—the feeling that it is breaking apart, that the two female characters are, from the dramatic point of view, not finished.

From this point on, the two female types are no longer actively opposed. The lyric, maidenly figure serves as a complement, or, like Sieglinde, as a preparatory figure, subsidiary to the other. Gutrune is a makeshift for the sake of the external development of the plot, which has, from the first sketch on, an unshakable center in

Brünnhilde. Also conceived under the inspiration of the personality of Schröder-Devrient, Brünnhilde is the center of the entire RING, which through her alone receives its reasonable justification. And just as Brünnhilde is the one truly active figure in the RING, so Isolde is in TRISTAN, Kundry in PARSIFAL, even Eva in MEISTERSINGER.

All the male figures are rooted in their relation to Woman, and from this relation they draw their life. They are important to the plot only to the degree of their relation to the central figure of woman. There are no contrasts, such as there were in Mozart, between men as nature and life create them. There is only a circle of lovers. Longing, desire, discernment, renunciation—all are expressed in many ways, to be sure: but every single figure is determined solely by his love-relationship to Woman.

Woman's individuality is unified in a single type representing the female of the species. There are changes in individual characterization, to be sure, from one work to another, but over and above all variations the type always remains Woman as singing creature of her sex. Man, on the other hand, is broken up into several rôles, this dissection, viewed from the dramatic standpoint, being the sensible exploitation of vocal differences provided by nature.

French opera had brought heroic extension particularly of the tenor and bass timbres, and German opera had emphasized the baritone for the expression of passionate beings driven by supernatural forces. In the title rôle of RIENZI Wagner sticks to the French model. But beginning with the HOLLÄNDER he creates beside the proper female type the two male voices: the baritone and tenor lovers. Both exist only through their relation to Senta, and are called forth by her existence. They present only in their difference a complete picture of man and his life, which proceeds from woman.

The further development of male vocal types in Wagner shows presentation of the male nature through tenor, baritone, and bass parts, with the accent now upon one, now upon another. Tenor and baritone, at least, are conceived throughout as complementary reflections of woman's nature in man. Tannhäuser and Wolfram; Lohengrin and the spurned Telramund; Siegmund, Siegfried, and Wotan; Sachs and Walter; Parsifal and Amfortas—they depend upon one another. In TRISTAN the distribution is outwardly changed by the scanty treatment of Melot, the limiting of Kurwenal to friendship for Tristan, above all through the incorporation of the bass rôle of Marke in the circle of lovers; but the basic attitude is the same. Paternal emotion, too, as exemplified in Daland, the Landgrave, König Heinrich, and Pogner, rests upon purified feelings of love.

It appears exalted to the plane of religion in Gurnemanz, and in its most striking inversion in Hagen.

The essential thing is not the degree or the variety of feeling for woman, but the fact that every male being depends for his existence solely upon that feeling. This is equally true of the diabolic figures: Alberich, who owes his power to the curse laid upon love; Loge, who tells of its mastery over the world; Klingsor, who mutilates himself in order to conquer it; Mime, who does not understand it; Beckmesser, who is made ridiculous by it; Hagen, who wishes to destroy it and thus destroys himself. Wherever the world of men appears it always proclaims *"lassen will nichts von Lieb' und Weib"* ("everything clings to woman and love"). Nor is the proclaiming all; for it is this idea which brought that world to life. Every turn of voice, every feature of its character is filled with the striving to give positive or negative expression to the thought of *"Weibeswonne und Wert"* ("the joy and worth of woman").*

Longing for woman demands of the vocal treatment that it exhibit all the qualities which promise fulfilment of that longing. Among these are brilliance and power —conquering radiance of tone; likewise the dark, the mysterious, the suffering, as it is described in Senta's ballad as the cause of feminine sympathy and devo-

* The quotations are from Loge's narrative in Scene 2 of DAS RHEINGOLD.

tion. Tenor and baritone, as Wagner forms them, are characterized by both these expressive opposites. In individual cases the boundaries are wiped out through expressive tension. Thus the tenor heroes Siegmund and Tristan—both suffering characters—are to a striking degree confined to the lower, almost baritone, registers.

Tonal expression is decisively influenced by the expression of speech. Wagner early achieved a deep realization of the importance of the speech problem in opera. His later writings hold fast, though with somewhat different deductions than in his youthful essays, to the idea that opera must be sung and that language must render the singing natural. Instinct and reflection lead Wagner to heed the root differences among languages and the differences in styles of singing which arise from them. Their physiological and climatic backgrounds, and the differences between styles of thought in the different languages, spring into prominence. Through recognition of the cultural roots of the problem he achieves the concept of verse-melody, which could be created only where the creator of words and music were one person. The words must carry the melody latent within them. It must have been heard, consciously or subconsciously, while they were being written, arising out of careful listening to the changing emotion of the words. And a fine ear for the latter could belong only to the person who had written the words and had creatively experienced the unexpressed something that determined their movement.

It is not conceivable that an Italian composer would ever have found it necessary to occupy himself with such reflections, but for the German musician they were unavoidable. Wagner's contrasting of the concepts "opera" and "drama" remains an only apparent antithesis, as long as a firm hold is kept on song as the expressive element. What Wagner demands of the opera, in contrast to the drama, is recognition of the necessities governing vocal style which arise out of the nature of the German language. This demand becomes inevitable the moment the voices sing original German words, with all the implied consequences as far as plot and text are concerned.

While Wagner worked out his own solution of the laws of tone related to language, he at first did nothing different from what Lortzing had already done, as he himself remarks. Probably Lortzing, within his modest sphere, had come up against the same difficulty and had thereupon written his own texts, without thinking too much about it. For Wagner the intellectual clarification was not to be avoided. His procedure could not help leading, in the field of tragic opera, to far-reaching consequences, as regards the subject matter and its development in his works, as well as the organic structure of the works. These consequences showed themselves most strikingly in the changed style of singing. Wagner was vigorously reproached for lack of melody, and therefore for an unsingable style.

Both objections are based upon the fact that Wagner substitutes German song-melody, based upon organic speech, for the accustomed instrumental melody. This was a new turning, not away from but towards song, which he again felt to be the natural sound of the human voice.

Experience shows that Wagner's speech-melody, which the ear admitted at first with such difficulty, has with time achieved a high degree of popularity. His vocal melody, it is true, underwent many changes. It began with the old operatic melody of RIENZI, which still showed a division, almost like Gluck's, into active, dramatic, and quieter lyric portions. With the HOLLÄNDER a hybrid style set in. Characteristic of this style is the duet between Senta and the Holländer, which begins in a pure, expressive, melodic line, and ends up in an Italianesque *stretta.* From this point on, song with Wagner becomes progressively freer. He gradually achieves a melodic style which, in clarity of outline and in intense compactness of expression, seems a transfigured reflection of old opera melody; the voices sing with a flexibility almost Italian in its ingratiating quality, while the declamatory line has a naturalistic plasticity. Speech and thought, the impulse of the action and the sound of the voice, are brought together in complete unity. What the German singing organ could create, in basic connection with the German language, is achieved. The dramatic symbols for the intellectual content and subject matter are found, and the dies for corresponding vocal types and characters are cast.

2

The development of speech-melody presupposes the predominance of the harmonic style, and of the orchestra as the bearer of this harmonic style. Here lay Wagner's basic difference from everything that had gone before: for song-melody, derived from speech, does away with the independence of the voice, making it a part of the instrumental sound-organism, whose support it constantly requires. The voices remain dramatic types of the most highly differentiated sort, but they are embedded in a coherent whole. The dramatic impulse becomes instrumental instead of vocal in character; it is primarily harmonic.

Hence arises the unique character of the subject matter of the plots. Plots concerning individuals, on the style of FIGARO or DON GIOVANNI, for example; realistic plays based upon ideas, like FIDELIO; even naïve folk-plots like that of the FREISCHÜTZ—none of these was possible upon such a foundation. The harmonic, instrumental medium of expression transfers the active impulse into the world of cosmic nature. The road to a drama of pure feeling is open, and the myth, centering upon the "purely human" personality, becomes the subject matter. At the same time a connection is established with that style of vocal characterization in which the female voice occupies a leading position and the men's voices group themselves around it as a center.

A consequence of all this, at first forced, is the expansion of the orchestral apparatus. Here, too, changes appear, affecting the multiplication of the instrumental body, the style of instrumentation, and the inner structure of the harmonic style, down to the most minute refinement of all modulatory, dynamic, and coloristic effects. Everything aims at making the harmony fluid. The most important means to this end is the *leit-motiv* technique. It is frequently considered an intellectualizing process, because externally it appears to be an essentially symphonic thematic device. In reality it is only the skeleton by means of which the harmonic organism functions.

In this connection it is apparent that Wagner used various modes of treatment at various times; and there is a similar variety in the subjects chosen and in their treatment. The middle group of works shows a considerable shrinking of the vocal apparatus. The number of singing voices is reduced to a minimum, long stretches of stage action are carried off by only two voices, monologue develops, long orchestral interludes are interpolated, every occasion for a set ensemble-piece for the voices is avoided. The singing chorus, which until then had been the very thing that stamped German romantic opera with its individual character, as it did French grand opera, has entirely disappeared. This contraction of the vocal forces applies, to be sure, only to the period between LOHENGRIN and TRISTAN, the period in which Wagner vigorously emphasized conscious opposition to former styles of singing, in theory as well as in practice. This conscious desire is further strengthened by his ever increasingly active harmonic style, which made itself felt in the orchestra with such irresistible force that it overwhelmed all singing elements and left only the strongest of them alive at all.

This exuberance over a newly-won consciousness is followed, after TRISTAN, by a return to the opera of large ensembles. Wagner had developed that type of opera up through LOHENGRIN; in MEISTERSINGER and GÖTTERDÄMMERUNG he took it up again, and in PARSIFAL he brought it to a conclusion. The ensemble of solo voices returns in the MEISTERSINGER quintet as a lyric, *concertante* conclusion. The chorus, and the finale which is built up out of it, are developed to a point that surpasses the older, romantic opera in power of individualization and the French grand opera in the intensity of its climaxes.

A man of the theatre like Wagner could, of course, for a time do without some of the means available for making his effect—for various reasons. When these reasons had disappeared, he had to take care to make all his forces again serve the ends he had in view. Always decisive for him is the goal. In such an opera the goal had to be the ensemble, in the most far-reaching sense. Its origin in harmonic action alone demanded that. For such harmonic action, a multiplicity of available forces was a premise, their interplay an organic requirement. The passing limitation to a small number of singers and the disappearance of the chorus were only apparent restrictions. They were compensated for by expansions in other directions. The idea of a great ensemble, in fact of the greatest possible ensemble, was inseparable from and basic to such an art-form. It makes little difference whether the ensemble is primarily vocal or, at times, instrumental. In any case, construction through climactic development is the central task. It corresponds to the nature of instrumental harmony, which is an ever-developing, ever-changing nature.

Hence arises Wagner's formal structure. The possibilities were the two-act type used in Mozart and *buffo* opera, the five-act mammoth type of grand opera, and the three-act form of romantic opera. Except in RIENZI,

Wagner decided on the three-act type. Now, it is not always possible so to compress the fullness of the story that the central portion—the second act—most succinctly illustrates the idea of the whole action. In this respect the middle act of the HOLLÄNDER is wholly successful. From Senta's Ballad right up to the chief number in the work—the duet between Senta and the Holländer—there runs an uninterrupted ascending line, which, while it exhibits all the active forces, makes clear with a sureness that seems almost supernatural the mutual awakening of the two characters to complete realization.

The second act of the HOLLÄNDER is the typical Wagner act. He later gave it several similar, and naturally more complicated, forms. Just as naturally, he at times more thoroughly explored the field of expression. But in its whole conception he never surpassed this middle act. In fact he failed in various cases—as in the second acts of LOHENGRIN and WALKÜRE, and the design of the RING as a whole—to achieve an equal unity.

The overloading in such cases is compensated for by a particularly tight first act. Perhaps it is in accord with some rule that the dynamic force of such opening acts as those of LOHENGRIN and WALKÜRE is followed by especially heavy-laden middle acts. It is also in accord with the law of change that the creative artist must ever alter his style of construction. But it is certain that Wagner's art shows its strongest side in those works in which, as in the HOLLÄNDER, the middle acts are really concentrated. In them Wagner realizes an equilibrium of all his creative and reflective forces, the integration and complementary balance of the voices and the supporting orchestral harmony. In these middle acts, in which all the active elements of the work flow together in a free union, the sense of the plot as well appears distilled down to its essence.

So the model of Wagner's harmoniously designed action consists of only one act. The two outer acts are necessary to the form, but as far as content is concerned they serve simply as preparation and conclusion to the action-carrying middle act. This framing significance of the two outer acts tells most clearly in PARSIFAL. As a formal structure, with its prelude and postlude in the first and third acts and its kernel in the second, PARSIFAL reveals the pure substance of Wagner's creative wisdom, just as the second act of the HOLLÄNDER shows it in its stormy, yet clear-seeing and exhaustive first manifestation.

But the most carefully balanced of all are TRISTAN and DIE MEISTERSINGER, throughout all their parts. Both works, dating from the years of creative maturity, always recognized, and rightly so, as Wagner's most perfect musical creations, claim absolute leadership in formal perfection as well. In them the three acts really stand in the relation of preparation, action, and fulfilment, which the three-act type requires. In both works the second act contains the quintessential idea, but this virtue is not purchased at the price of any lack in the other parts. The first act of TRISTAN, like that of LOHENGRIN or DIE WALKÜRE, is among the greatest pieces of exposition known to the musical stage. The opening and closing acts of the MEISTERSINGER preserve throughout, despite the exceptional length of the last act, an acute and tight coherence. As if celebrating a returning joy in the most joyous form of play, even the dance—not admitted by Wagner as a separate scenic episode since RIENZI—here celebrates its resurrection.

Among Wagner's operas, TANNHÄUSER alone is an exception. It is his most remarkable work, and he never quite finished with it. The conception of the double character of Elisabeth-Venus is not the only remarkable thing in it. Tannhäuser himself is Wagner's most ambiguous male character, and at the same time the one closest to life. He is the strongest of the tenors, like Sachs among the baritones and Hagen among the basses. These three may be said to represent together the complete man; all the others may be classified under the headings for which these three stand. But even Sachs and Hagen cannot be compared with Tannhäuser in problematic significance. In him Wagner attempted to sum up man as comprehensively as he had woman in Senta. With woman this attempt could succeed, because it sprang from a basic desire. With man it was not successful. Thus this character was forever dividing up into its components. It created its own counterpart in Lohengrin, it went through the various metamorphoses of the RING characters, yielded a portion of its passionate nature to the baritone, grew into Tristan, and finally found rest in the double character of Parsifal-Amfortas, just as Venus did in Kundry.

But in TANNHÄUSER—the bold, ground-breaking work of early manhood—unfinished so far as the sense goes, inner unrest is mirrored. The work had two centers, just as it was dominated by two women's voices: the big finale of the second act and the Venusberg scene in the first. The two remain forever side by side unreconciled. Wagner later underlined in the Paris version the significance of the Venusberg, which had at first been restrained. In the Paris version he created the third of those great duet acts—the other two being the final act of SIEGFRIED and the middle act of PARSIFAL—in which the middle act of the HOLLÄNDER is brought to fulfilment. Here he formulated everything which, according to his conception of the German voice singing in German, it was possible to formulate: the call of love. It is the language of the emotions, lifted out of the sphere of purely human experience, carried forward by the harmonic activity in the orchestra.

3

For his characters, Wagner always had singing actors in mind. His primary emphasis upon the acting was directed in critical opposition to the dramatically untutored singer. It would never have occurred to him to sacrifice the singing voice. He simply did not want the *bel canto* singer of vocal melodies for their own sake. He had in mind creatures of universal gifts, who would sing just as well as they spoke and acted. In fact the requirement of universality was not limited to the protagonists: it applied to every factor in the production. It called for the mobilization of all forces, of a perfect ensemble in the broadest sense.

To Wagner's ensemble belong not only the actors taking part, but all the optical and acoustical forces that contribute to the impression—even those involving only the spectator, affecting his repose and his ability to concentrate: darkening of the theatre, arrangement of the seats so that all could see equally well, placing of the orchestra below the stage. All these are the consequences of Wagner's central thought: the action. All are based upon one essential requirement: illusion.

Illusion is a higher reality, in the sense that it depicts true nature, purged of all the petty details of life.

Illusion in this sense reaches far beyond the proscenium in the working out of its action. In creating something real out of stage-play it demands of the spectator faith and active participation as the last step in the production of its effect.

The singing voice, as original point of departure for this theatrical orgy, seems forgotten. It has been transformed into German speech-melody. In ever further-reaching effect, it has pressed into its service every vocal, instrumental, and scenic device. It has finally drawn the hearer himself into the play and made him a part of its ensemble. Out of action and illusion, the fantasy-picture of a complete art-work has arisen, "the work of music made visible."

That is the ensemble idea in essence: the drawing of the spectator into the theatrical circle as an integral, participating "final cause." It is also the means of making the vocal play of the opera live for the German, not primarily gifted for song, and of enabling him to become productive, through this common experience, in the world of tone and song. It demonstrates the possibility of German opera in a special, national form corresponding to Italian and French models. This form then adapts itself to international circulation because it contains within itself all previous forms of European Opera, transformed and placed in fruitful relation to the idea of the whole.

The vocal types that appear in it, however, become new human types, according to their behavior. Their confinement to the sphere of feeling, and their individualization according to the degree of their emotional intensity, gives an indication, beyond the limitations of musical structure, of the nature of the general culture of the time. The conception of woman as the active center of life finds its corresponding echo in the basic conceptions of the intellectual life of the period.

Thus German opera grows, out of what appear at first to be confining limitations, to have a world significance such as had once belonged to Italian opera as an art creation and later to French grand opera as a creation of society. While German opera takes unto itself all the elements of grand opera, and by its creative treatment gives them artistic unity, it stands nevertheless in sharp contrast to grand opera. Grand opera has but the one attraction of its virtuosity to present, and then is pressed into a defensive and hopeless position.

It is otherwise with Italian opera. It, too, seemed, in passing, to be eclipsed and pushed aside by the idea of the comprehensive art-work. But the day came when the accompanying intellectual attitude, which had given this many-sided art its ethical and cultural aura, itself subsided. Thereupon the opera, and with it the aged and eternal basic power of the singing voice as the proper life-form of this comprehensive art, became clearly recognizable again. Then the longing reawoke for the original, natural sound of the human voice. This was the time when Wagner's works were first really understood in their extraordinary artistic significance.

Simultaneously, the beauty characteristic of the Italian voice reappears. Recognition of song-opera as the original form of opera is reawakened to new life in its native land. This recognition is achieved, proclaimed, and finally made current throughout Europe, by Verdi.

Chapter IX

VERDI

VERDI was born in the same year as Wagner, 1813, and survived him by eighteen years. Like Wagner, Verdi wrote almost nothing but operas, his other works being few and episodic. He wrote twenty-six operas, twice as many as Wagner, if the latter's youthful operas are counted in among his works.

The difference is not explainable by Verdi's longer life-span, for after Wagner's death Verdi published only two operas. Nor may we assume such fluency or immense superficiality in Verdi as would have made quicker work possible to him. Nor yet does the difference in the number of works produced by the two men arise from any greater conscientiousness of either towards his work. It is in fact based upon the difference in their mental attitude towards the nature of opera.

For Wagner, opera is first of all a problem. Dramatic singing in an unvocal language with brittle voices necessitates an extra amount of reflection, which Verdi neither needs nor knows. He writes his unproblematic, Italian song-opera, which is closely connected with the practical works of Bellini, Mercadante, and Donizetti, and is intended for performance in Milan, Naples, or the Italian provinces. It is active art, unhampered by thought.

Verdi, besides, is not a man of culture, like Wagner. Everything of literary or aesthetically speculative nature is foreign to him. He is not an intellectually active man of the middle class; he is a peasant rooted in the soil, and he carries this primitive quality over into his art.

The young Verdi is widely considered to have been a rough and raw fellow, particularly because of his occasionally almost brutal temperament. Verdi was, indeed, a deeply passionate nature, and a fundamentally masculine one—in fact, one of the most masculine figures in the history of art. The inimitable part of his artistic achievement consists not least in this masculinity, doubly impressive because of its rarity. That the first utterances of such a nature should seem to the culture of an overrefined period crude, banal, or even of street-ballad type, is not Verdi's fault. He never altered this basic trait of his nature, even in his later utterances, which were, to be sure, less primitive.

Such a combination—a masculine personality, rooted in the soil—was bound to be reflected in his choice of texts. Verdi at first pays little attention to mere anecdotal subject matter. It is the ideological background implied in a text that is decisive for him. His peasant nature required an ideology in which concepts of freedom, fatherland, unity, were combined with heroic masculinity. For the rest, variety of color in subject and setting predominates. He did not seek after nationalistic allusions but rather avoided them as dangerous. But such ideas are continually breaking through at the proper moment; they are the tie that binds the many and varied externals together. At the same time, the national language-spirit works itself out in the new Italian opera, too: it relates the passions of individuals to general ideas, out of which on every possible occasion national catch-phrases for the desires and aims of a people blaze forth.

From this basic standpoint, then, the libretto is considered according to varying taste and requirements. As in French opera, the entertainment value of the subject matter and of the structure of the action acquires more and more significance: the character of the subject matter decides the fate of the opera. These are conditions that remind us of the increased importance of the linguistic, intellectual, conceptual elements of the opera. They show that the change that sets in with the increased nationalizing of German and French opera affects Italian opera, too, even though the vocabulary

PORTRAIT DE VERDI

and the natural relation of the language to song-tones remain unchanged.

Verdi sought to meet the requirement of variety of action in opera by paying close attention to narrative and dramatic literature. He is the first musician to solve the problem in this obvious fashion. It was a question not of requiring the text to be of higher literary quality, but only of giving it mobility, variety, character. What was needed was some tension in the action instead of a simple adaptability to music; a dramatically climactic construction instead of a simple, consecutive musical arrangement. This was a change only of libretto *methods,* not of libretto *values;* the latter remained unaffected by the change.

Verdi received his most important artistic stimuli from works of Victor Hugo, Schiller, and Shakespeare. He also used subjects from the novels of Dumas and other, lesser known writers. Verdi, then, showed clearly what he desired in the increasing certainty with which he governed the choice and the treatment of his texts. His relations to his subjects and librettos are just as illuminating as are Wagner's to his, different as the two worlds are.

This difference shows itself strikingly in the relation of the two composers to grand opera. Wagner, after a short novitiate, feels himself drawn to it because the state of German opera leaves him no other choice. For

Verdi this motive does not exist. The Italian stage, when Verdi made his appearance, was influenced, to be sure, by Paris, capital of Europe at the time; but still, thanks to favorable circumstances, it continued to exist as an independent institution, preserving for the native musician genuine possibilities of expansion. Only after he had written eighteen Italian operas and was already forty years old, did Verdi write his first grand opera for Paris, I VESPRI SICILIANI, then to continue the series with five other big works in the fifteen years that lead to AÏDA. The motives that brought him to this form—a form always fascinating because of its variety—do not consist exclusively of details of artistic conception. AÏDA is not conceivable without Meyerbeer's L'AFRICAINE—at least not in such rich and conclusive maturity—and the after-effects of its melodic and rhythmic style are apparent right up through OTELLO.

But despite the significance of grand opera for Verdi, it remained only a bridge. He did not change it, like Wagner, into a form to fit his needs. He ended by leaving it altogether and returning to his native ground. His fifteen-year pause after AÏDA, his preoccupation during this pause with extra-theatrical works—mostly vocal, but including a string quartet—are not to be explained as resulting from the assimilation of Wagnerian influences. Of course Verdi received food for thought from Wagner, but any influence in the often accepted sense was not possible. Verdi recognized better than anyone else the limitations of Wagner's works arising as they did out of the world of thought and language.

On the other hand, Wagner's influence may have helped to hasten Verdi's day of reckoning with grand opera. The outcome of his giving up this form was the creating of the two last works of Italian opera: a last *seria,* OTELLO, a last *buffa,* FALSTAFF. Both, like Wagner's works, are concluding phenomena of a period of culture. They do not, to be sure, cut off the possibility of further creation. But as documents of a unified artistic, historical, and cultural maturity which was most highly individual, they present a total which for a considerable time cannot be surpassed or indeed approached.

To the basic ideology of the text, to the enhanced importance of all qualities deriving from language, corresponds Verdi's desire for generalization of vocal types. These types return again and again. Human beings divide, according to their voices, into several basic categories. But these categories—and here Verdi's opera differs from the old song-opera—are character-groups. Their vocal classification follows upon the recognition of their character, which is primary.

Verdi follows this principle from the beginning of his work, most strikingly in the conspicuous place he gives to the baritone. The voice is like the ancient character-mask and the baritone is the protagonist. Of the great Italian masters until that time, only Rossini had favored the baritone. In the Figaro of the BARBER, he had created the model buffo-baritone as in Tell he had created the model for all Italian dramatic baritone figures. Verdi goes right on from this point, and his relation to Rossini is closest in this moulding of his central figures out of the baritone voice. Hereafter all his works are traversed by the same basic lines: Oberto, Nabucco, Carlos in ERNANI, Macbeth, and the other central baritone figures of his early period; then Rigoletto, Luna, Germont père, Boccanegra, René in UN BALLO IN MASCHERA, Carlos and Posa in LA FORZA DEL DESTINO, and Amonasro, right up to the culminating figures in the tragic and *buffo* domains, Iago and Falstaff.

The baritone is the basic theme of Verdi's opera. It becomes heroic, lyric, elegiac, brutal, lordly, possessed, and is developed to the highest pitch of expression. But it is never passive—always active, leading. The power of the baritone is the creative and motive power of the male, is in fact man himself. Man in Verdi's world is not a lover. He is something much more important—he is the producer of the action. Herein lies the difference between Wagner and Verdi: as Wagner's art turns about the central figure of woman, so Verdi's art moves around the figure and nature of man and the male voice.

Among all Verdi's leading baritone figures, not one is a lover, unless Luna and the René of UN BALLO IN MASCHERA—the one rejected, the other deceived—are regarded as lovers. The rest are fathers, like Miller, Rigoletto, Germont, Amonasro; friends, like Carlos and Posa; kings, like Nabucco, Attila, Macbeth; or sinister or grotesque figures like Francesco Moor, Iago, Falstaff. They are men whose existence is independent of woman. They are elemental forces, prototypes of the masculine—somehow of the absolute creative as well. They rise out of the sphere of erotic desire and exemplify the truly heroic. Verdi, animated by this basic impulse, breaks through the circle of the play of the sexes, drawn by Mozart, and of the consequent relations between the voices of man and woman. He restores the one male singer to the center of the action, all the other forces moving about it. The baritone thus achieves the organic formal significance once held by the *castrato* voice, but in enhanced form, since it does not contradict nature. Only now it can sing again without thought of erotic purpose. It proclaims only the basic will to plastic characterization of a human prototype through the one voice suited to this purpose—the masculine voice of medium register.

By placing the baritone in the center of the tonal

action, Verdi changed the significance of the opera from action concerned primarily with love to action concerned primarily with character. In this process, the importance of the tenor-lover was bound to diminish. In all matters of action the tenor is led by the baritone: Othello by Iago, Carlos by Posa, Alfredo by the father, who, although he is not prominent externally, is still the driving force of the action. At other times, the tenor is a colleague, apparently superior, but in reality not equal—like the Duke in RIGOLETTO. Occasionally the relation of the voices is shifted by the addition of a bass, who, always conceived as an old man, is given as a lover a sort of tragic, fatalistic treatment, like Silva in ERNANI and King Philip in DON CARLOS.

For Verdi the tone of the tenor voice has no style-determining character. It has brilliance and bravura lightness, combined with accents of heroic force and temperamental spontaneity. Externally radiant, but essentially frail, it remains the shuttlecock of opposing forces, always subordinated as a dramatic unit to the pensive baritone. The tenor needs to be complemented by a woman's voice. It is a duet-voice, not a solo-voice—like the lyric soprano that completes it.

This lyric soprano appears in many varieties: from the light, bravura voice of Leonora in IL TROVATORE, full of coloratura virtuosity, through the pure coloratura types of Gilda and Violetta, and the expressive, lyrically intense voices of Amelia, Elisabetta, and Aïda, to the tender and elegiac Desdemona. But like the tenor, the lyric soprano, beautifully as Verdi knows how to write for it, with all the paternal affection he bestows on it, and with all its significance in the scheme of the whole, plays no leading part. Verdi's vocal scheme requires operas containing two women, like Wagner's TANNHÄUSER and LOHENGRIN. Yet his approach to the female voice has nothing to do with Wagner's. Verdi's two-woman operas are foreshadowed by Bellini—as is his baritone by Rossini—most expressively in Norma and Adalgisa: the light, youthful high soprano, contrasted with the fuller, dramatic mezzo which Bellini still decked out with rich ornamentation harking back to the old dramatic coloratura type of singer. Verdi gradually deepens the tone until he is writing chiefly for the medium register. For him this vocal type becomes the counterpart of the baritone. He needs woman for her temperament, needs her as the reservoir which nature has particularly appointed for the passions.

Thus arises the series of female types of heroic cast who in Verdi's works actually play opposite the men—not giving them wings, but limiting them, pinning them down to earth. Among these belong Abigail in NABUCCO; Lady Macbeth; Azucena, who assumes almost sibylline greatness, and close to her, although like Maddalena in RIGOLETTO only an episodic figure; Ulrica in UN BALLO IN MASCHERA; and finally the two magnificently conceived fulfilments of the series, Eboli and Amneris, who close the list of Verdi's dramatically active woman-characters. Emilia in OTELLO is only an accompanying figure, and in FALSTAFF there is only Quickly as a sort of humorous foil.

All these women are creatures of passion. They manifest love for men only so far as it acts as a motive for jealousy. Their action awakens, far beyond the realm of erotic feeling, life's darker forces—will to power, desire for combat, thirst for revenge—and thus sets in opposition to the upward striving of man the fatally earth-bound nature of woman. To Verdi, whose attitude was thoroughly masculine, woman is pleasing only in her weaker aspects. As the female of the species, she is the downward-drawing force, driven by the power of the blood, and seeking, as the earth-bound element, to force man's will down to her own level. From this point of view Verdi sees man and woman not as a pair of lovers but as primitive, opposing forces.

This is the kernel of the drama as Verdi's nature grasps it, and as it presents itself to him with ever-increasing clarity. In some operas the male and in some the female characters predominate. Verdi follows no planned scheme, yet his every thought can produce but these elements. At times the basic types are juxtaposed, like Macbeth and Lady Macbeth; at times, on the other hand, only one of them is present, like Iago. For the most part they represent the poles of the action, which do not come into direct contact with one another but are nevertheless the underlying forces: Azucena and Luna, Eboli and Posa, Amneris and Amonasro. Their field of force is the world of creatures of love desiring and seeking each other; the tenor and soprano each needing its complement; the two suffering their fate, not determining it; imprisoned, doomed, poisoned, buried alive. They are the weak ones, lyric even when they represent heroic characters like Rhadames, and the *bel canto* singers who, like Ernani, make away with themselves at the command of the controlling power. From the early works to OTELLO there is a single unified line of passive heroism, vain resistance to superior powers. Only the Duke in RIGOLETTO is an exception. He stands above the fate that here befalls the supposedly directing figure of the baritone. Thus the constellations change in detail, and upon this change rests the attraction of variety, ever anew spurring on the musician's fancy to produce new creative ideas.

Verdi's was an essentially new approach to the problem. By relegating to second place the erotic play between man and woman as a motivating impulse, making it only an object of the action, and making this action itself consist in the juxtaposition of two elemental character forces, Verdi takes away the erotic impulse that had determined the character of melody since Mozart. In its place he sets character-melody, melody without sex attraction, melody arising purely out of the action of the singers, as a spontaneous outburst of energy from the action itself. Verdi's melody thus attains a vital directness whose full-blooded objectiveness may at first seem occasionally almost coarse. Declamation as such plays at first a subordinate rôle; it is the curve, the buoyancy, the rhythmic power of the vocal melodic line that is decisive. Together with these, Verdi's melody has another new quality: its close relation to the immediate present. It is no mere construction planned from a distance on a purely artistic basis. It comes into being at the very moment it is sung. It is a directly illustrative event: it is the melodic form taken by the emotion just experienced. It is not meditative, reflective, pictorial; it does not refer to what has gone before. It grows out of the moment.

Upon this fact rests not only Verdi's unexampled intensity of stage effect, but concomitantly the justification of his choice of subjects. These seem to be only series of occasions for emotion. And that is the intention behind them. The literary element, although carefully treated, is without importance in itself. When Verdi uses literary texts, he strips them of their literary quality. He does not aim to set Shakespeare, Schiller, Hugo, to music; he expects them only to provide him with opera-subjects and plots. Emotions of the moment, arising from high tensions and agitations, following one another with organically increasing intensity, continuously spurring the characters on—such are the needs of his art. It thus goes back quite consciously to the most primitive essentials of the theatre, aims at the effect of improvisation, and therefore avoids everything self-consciously artistic. All problems of an intellectual nature are similarly avoided. With such a point of view they would not be possible, and, furthermore, they lie entirely outside the intentions of an art which concerns itself only with the primitive and the elementary both in its basic ideas and in the form it gives to them.

This art strove to become ever broader and more popular. It could easily afford in the process to lay itself open to the reproach of banality, a reproach no more genuine than that of the alleged back-stairs romanticism of the texts. Its very nature compelled it to strive to emerge from the individual and subjective to the general. Characteristic is the fact that, in Verdi's earliest works, the choruses—and among them several written in unison—make the greatest effect. The "Va pensiero" chorus in NABUCCO is particularly illuminating in this respect, but all the works of this period show similar traits. Verdi's path leads from this broad choral melody, at first sung by the mass, through gradual division, interweaving, and loosening of the melodic texture, to ever subtler melodic organization. The more transparently the task is set, the more the melodic language crystallizes, though never denying its origin. Verdi never becomes over-refined, but his eye gains in discrimination and penetration. The richer his view of the world of appearances, the richer the flow of his melody. And in this process the word plays a leading part. Language penetrates the musical texture and forms it into ever finer shapes, not through declamatory treatment, but through spiritual organization, sensuous moulding, and architectural broadening of the melodic substance.

Upon the same foundation Verdi built his ensembles. Ensembles in the grand style, in the Mozartean sense, had existed only in Rossini and in the older *opera buffa,* while the ensembles of Bellini, Mercadante, and Donizetti are limited to harmonic support and enhancement of a leading voice. Rossini is the first whose ensembles produce several independent vocal types out of the organic relation of many voices sounding together. But while Rossini's ensemble evolves toward unification, a unison of voices, Verdi preserves individual characters as such. He reveals himself in the combining of melodies in his own individual style. Here is an inner relation between his ensemble style and Mozart's, although

Verdi's goal is always the expansion of melody as expressive of character, while in Mozart it is the voice as an instrument of song that dominates.

Verdi's duets and trios are, like his arias, for the most part essential parts of the action—mutual incitation especially of the voices that belong together, like soprano and tenor. Only in this relation do the voices really succeed in fully projecting themselves in song, as in the great duets of TRAVIATA, AÏDA, and OTELLO. Here the direct actuality of Verdi's song asserts itself in the blending of voices of different register in the same emotional line. The final duet of Aïda and Rhadames shows this art of vocal dramaturgy in just as perfect a form as the great first-act duet of Desdemona and Otello. But besides these concerted pieces that are part of the plot there is in almost all Verdi's operas another solo-ensemble, marking a standstill in the action that is yet a gathering together of all the principal vocal characters. This simultaneity of various elements, which represents the placing beside each other in the music of elements that succeed each other in the action, effects a special intensification of the tonal constituents of the drama.

This ensemble is the Verdi quartet, as it exists most clearly in RIGOLETTO, DON CARLOS, and OTELLO. It is the key to Verdi's musical and vocal dramaturgy. It brings the chief characters together, exhibiting the special characteristics of each and simultaneously the relations to and dependence of each upon the others. It denotes the spiritual course of the plot, in that it reveals the moving forces and makes clear their basic relations. It discloses the world of each opera as the relation between these forces. The vocal quartet is for Verdi the ideal picture of a totality of sound. By gathering together the leading and conflicting elements, it creates the illusion of an entity above all individual differences of sex and personality, in which all human powers of singing are united, but without the limitations that attend every individual example of such powers.

Verdi never exceeded the four voices of the quartet in his solo-ensembles. From it he passed directly to the mass-ensemble, the chorus. For him, especially in the earlier works, the chorus equally with the soloists is the bearer of the melody. From the dramaturgic viewpoint, we may say that the chorus is an independent element of the narrative as of the tonal action. Hence Verdi's preference for a unison treatment of the chorus; hence also his frequent division into men's and women's voices, either juxtaposed, as in the second finale of Il Trovatore, or, as in other works right up to and including the choruses of Otello, building up to a climax by a purely tonal changing back and forth between them. He also likes to use the men's chorus for narratives, for conspiracy scenes, for whispering intermezzi.

With the turning towards grand opera, the importance of the chorus in the plot becomes less than its significance as a dynamic means for the construction of mass effects. Here the dance element of the grand opera penetrates into Verdi's work, although it does not really belong there and never becomes quite at home. Verdi's ballet music always retains the character of interpolation. The dance becomes a living thing for him only in those places where it is closely related to the musical action: in the introductory minuet of RIGOLETTO; in the TRAVIATA waltz; in the death minuet of UN BALLO IN MASCHERA.

Verdi used mass-ensembles most effectively and definitively in the AÏDA March. They are among his most popular, but artistically least independent, creations. From the point of view of the plot they are superimposed, and they have accordingly an almost cantata-like character. They display Verdi's characteristic tonal imagination and rhythmic energy, plus the art, based upon Meyerbeer's models, of decorative construction. The finale as a climax achieved by massed voices, however, does not fit Verdi's tonal scheme. Ensembles for him belong in the middle of the act. They act as reservoirs from which the individual figures that follow are supplied. The economy of the entire scheme of OTELLO is characteristic: the coördinate insertion of the chorus, and the breaking off of the climax of the only big ensemble-finale (that of the third act), which dies away into distant cries of the chorus.

With Wagner the development is exactly inverted: everything tends to dissolve in the harmony, so that PARSIFAL becomes another chorus-opera in a comprehensive sense. With Verdi, the ever more subtly adjusted harmony is constantly branching out into melodic line: out of the tonal complex of the big ensemble arises ever anew the solo voice.

Verdi's orchestra undergoes a similar course of development. It is and remains subordinate to the singer. But it is less bearer of the harmony, as in Wagner, than a means of establishing and pointing the rhythm and thus the tempo of the action. To that extent it does not accompany the voice; it leads it. It gives the melody body, actuality, movement. Even more: it gives the voice its melody. The introduction to a Verdi aria gives the impression not so much of a prelude as of the source from which the melody arises. Thus the orchestra—even in Verdi's earliest works—is more a partner of the voice than its accompanist; not as a juxtaposed element, to be sure, but as a harmonic and rhythmic complement of the voice. In this respect, too, Verdi remains himself throughout his life. The evolution is only the progress of an ever more refined discrimination, the laying bare of the system of veins and arteries that seems to shine out of the block of marble in all its intricate ramifications so as to make the material seem so transparent as to be overlooked. Word and thought are the chisels that make possible this process of revealing the elemental complex of sound.

Thus Verdi's path leads from the old opera of set pieces to the final works: OTELLO and FALSTAFF. This road leads to no climax in the customary sense. It is a path that is broad at first and narrow at the end, a path to a height where the air is thinner. Elemental impulses of human nature, love, jealousy, wickedness, stupidity, make themselves heard. They sing out of the voices with an inner freedom of melodic conformation that is beyond all convention. They sing out of tenor, soprano, and baritone voices as if these vocal ranges themselves were definitely conclusive—as if one need only classify men according to the categories of their voices, in order to reach final knowledge of their characters.

In OTELLO this creative principle is carried out in tragedy, in FALSTAFF in comedy. In OTELLO, therefore, Verdi arrives at a conclusive embodiment of the basic vocal types as individual characters, while in FALSTAFF he attains a classification of more than individual variety, represented among the soloists by the double quartet of men's and women's voices, and multiplied in the tones of the chorus. This is a method of creating a chorus by splitting up the voices into ever smaller groups, which then, in the Fugue of the Fools, are unified again, always grouped about the leading baritone as the core.

In FALSTAFF, Verdi's art of vocal melody reaches its climax in the final ensemble. This is not, like the Wagner ensemble, an organized assembling of a multiplicity of heterogeneous forces. Its musical symbol is the basic form of the old polyphony: the fugue. It is a primary unity, which appears to be divided without ever losing its inner connection. This unity arises from a melodic idiom based on the single vocal type of Falstaff representing man as fool, ever changing, donning now the tragic and now the comic mask, appearing now as man and now as woman, but behind all these appearances remaining always the same primitive being. The fugue subject is presented in all its varying forms by the singing voice. Any individual disguise is lacking. There remain only voices of all registers, throwing the same theme back and forth among themselves until this variety itself leads back into the final unity.

But all this remains within the bounds of song. There is no drawing of the spectator into the action, no direct participation by the audience. The concept of the whole is kept firmly within musical limits. It embraces the scenic element as an extra device. Stage-setting in Verdi is mere illustrative decoration of the events of the action. He makes only modest demands upon it, limited to insignificant aids to the illusion, of which the most important requirement is that they should be unobtrusive. This loose connection with the decorative frame is changed in those works that were written as grand operas, which purposely made use of scenic devices. In them, the decorative element is also consciously taken over into the music. This is true especially of Aïda, which has a definite national coloring. In his other operas Verdi makes no distinction between men of different places: whether they are French, Spanish, Scotch, or German, their melodies remain as Italian as the passions by which they are moved.

There is therefore no special *milieu,* no individual atmosphere belonging to a particular subject. Verdi's opera is character-opera. It contains only characters, which are to be made clear as such. The most important part of this task is achieved through song. The figure of the protagonist, in fact everything human that moves upon the stage, must correspond to the singing. The style of the action is determined by the absolutely present-day quality of Verdi's characterization. Verdi is a realist; he gives no explanation or interpretation, nothing but the simple fact, the event, the human being himself in the most spare and direct form. He assumes the natural vitality of the good Italian actor who knows how to illustrate the action without pursuing psychological studies. There are in Verdi no problematic characters; there can be none, according to the nature of his art. Those that existed in the material he used, he simplified. Nothing else is possible to a dramatist who works with only three or four basic types throughout a long life. Verdi had no more at his disposal because human voices provided him with no more.

Verdi's work, like every creative product arising out of the limitations of a national tongue, was for a long time open to misunderstanding. It was asking a great deal of the contemporaries of Wagner and Verdi to absorb both of them at once. False comparisons, with all the consequent false conclusions, were not to be avoided. They resulted, when recognition of song as the essence of opera was again achieved, in Verdi's being preferred to Wagner, after the relation had been exactly the opposite, and with as little justification. But comparisons merely hinder the effort to understand both figures. The national limitations of language and the spirit of language are at the root of the creative activity of both. For both there was a second general limitation in the nature of the national protagonist, conceived by Wagner as a singing actor and by Verdi as a sounding voice. The fact that Wagner's conception was bound up with the figure of a woman of genius as he had met it in the person of Schröder-Devrient, while Verdi placed the baritone itself, the most masculine of men's voices, at the center of his musical hearing, only confirms the diametrical contrast between the two natures and the two types of art, which meet only in their goal.

Wagner brings out every bit of singing ability that exists in the German, employing the lever of instrumental and scenic representation, unifying the whole by the fiction of a dramatic goal. Verdi adapts the beauty of Italian song to action. The vitalizing of the voice, the creation of actual, alive melody is his achievement. Thus he separates himself from the studio opera-melody of the time that had preceded him, and gives melody the actuality of *plein-air* painting.

In these two figures, the greatest artistic forces of the entire 19th century, German and Italian opera had set up models that seemed to exhaust all conceivable possibilities of the two cultures. The only thing remaining to complete the romantic opera of the middle class was the final contribution of French opera, which, after the cosmopolitan type of grand opera, now created the French model for this period, based on national languages.

Chapter X

LYRIC OPERA

Gounod *Thomas* *Bizet* *Offenbach*
Massenet *Mascagni* *Leoncavallo*
Puccini *Moussorgsky* *Debussy*

I

WHILE Wagner in Germany and Verdi in Italy were perfecting the national operas based upon their respective languages, there arose in France a new species: lyric opera. Beginning as a sort of hybrid, halfway between grand opera and *opéra-comique,* it soon acquired so firm a footing that it became the representative of French composition, attracted to itself the most important national gifts, and gradually drew foreign countries as well into its orbit: not alone Italy but the Slavic countries as well, which now began to take part in the creation of operas.

The life-spans of the older composers of this lyric opera correspond approximately to those of Wagner and Verdi; the youngest reach the apex of their creative activity about the turn of the century. Ambroise Thomas was born in 1811, Gounod in 1818, Offenbach in 1819, Smetana in 1824, Saint-Saëns and Moussorgsky in 1825, Bizet in 1838, Massenet in 1842. These are the older generation. Sixteen years pass before the births of Puccini and Leoncavallo in 1858; Charpentier follows in 1860, Debussy in 1862, Mascagni in 1863, Dukas in 1865. The chronology of their outstanding works corresponds only roughly to the composers' birth-dates. The first typical work of the lyric species is Gounod's FAUST, produced in 1859. MIGNON appears in 1866, and THE BARTERED BRIDE in the same year; Moussorgsky's BORIS in 1874, CARMEN in 1875. Six years later (1881) comes the LES CONTES D'HOFFMANN; Massenet's MANON and Puccini's WILLIS date from 1884; SAMSON from 1887, CAVALLERIA RUSTICANA from 1890, PAGLIACCI from 1892, Puccini's MANON LESCAUT from 1893, BOHÈME from 1896, TOSCA and Charpentier's LOUISE from 1900, Debussy's PELLÉAS ET MÉLISANDE from 1902, MADAMA BUTTERFLY from 1904, Dukas's ARIANE ET BARBE-BLEUE from 1907, followed by Puccini's one-act operas and his TURANDOT.

The chronology is important. It shows the growth from many sources of what is, despite many individual differences, an essentially unified species; its coming to the fore in the period after Wagner's death and during the last years of Verdi's life, its domination, based upon world-wide successes, about the turn of the century, and finally the extinction of the impulse that brought it to life. It shows the overlapping of French lyric opera into the Italian field after Verdi, although in this connection the earlier influence of Verdi upon the French lyric-opera composers is not to be overlooked. Thus influence from the one direction is repaid with influence from the other, all the more strikingly when Verdi, from OTELLO on, takes back the leadership of the new Italian opera and the works of the young Italians lean as much upon OTELLO as upon CARMEN and French lyric opera.

Common to the entire series, in addition to the organic connections among its members, is their inner attitude towards Wagner. As his influence began to be felt, Wagner was much watched and much discussed as a spiritual and artistic phenomenon; but his influence was productive only in the musical field. Not only Wagner, with his idea of rooting the action in the instrumental harmony, met with growing opposition: the older form of grand opera was also rejected. In those of the new works in which it did appear—in SAMSON, and in several works of Massenet—it was at first stripped of its virtuoso brilliance, brought back to a somewhat more serious musical point of view. But this robs it of some of its original character and keeps it from being completely representative of the species. One may say that after Meyerbeer's L'AFRICAINE no more grand operas were written, and that this final work of the most important master of the species was also the final work of the species itself.

Grand opera had starved on a diet of cosmopolitan virtuosity. National creative forces in France were striving for realization in a frame which, without achieving the dimensions of grand opera, nevertheless exceeded those of the *comique*. The emotional element was pressing forward and demanding emphasis of lyricism as the original basic character of French opera. The influence of Italian *buffa* had limited this attitude, had pointed the way to a development of the lyric element into the heroic pathos of grand opera, admitting sentiment in the *comique* only as a secondary feature. Here was the most important source of expression for French musical creation, and for the French singing voice, small and delicate, to be sure, but capable of subtle modulation, possessing a timbre appropriate to lyric expression, and counting agility and power of plastic accentuation among its virtues. The closer the connection became between speech and song, in the pathos and virtuosity of grand opera as well as in the dramatic penetration of the singing style of the *comique*, the more pressing became the desire to use these achievements in the technique of speech and song in a form both serious and yet wholly suited to French voices and language-potentialities.

The lyric tenor, with the light high register, coloratura abilities, and lyric delicacy of expression, had been created in its complete form in the *comique:* beyond George Brown nothing further was possible, vocally speaking. But the dramatic possibilities were not exhausted. For these two things had hitherto been lacking: feminine complement and a counter-rôle of equal importance. The French female voice is in temperament that of the soubrette. It is versatile. It can treat the higher registers in a light, engaging style, or it can give them color. It has the possibility of a sonorous middle register, which because of Romance phonetics sounds almost like an alto. In this respect it resembles the Italian mezzo-soprano. Without possessing the expansive possibilities of the latter in dramatic cantabile singing, it is equally plastic in the interpretation of a melodic speech-line. This vocal type, capable of development in two directions, needed only an inner emotional intensification in order to leave the domain of light, conversational style for that of serious lyric or dramatic song. The third basic type was the increasingly important one of the lyric baritone. It does not reach the primitive force of the Verdi baritone, nor yet the intense masculinity of the baritones of Wagner, but it possesses a beautiful, smooth, soft tone, and is capable, at the same time, of considerable force. The basic character of these three vocal types remained necessarily within the field of lyric expression.

Apart from all questions of voice and singing style, they likewise suited perfectly the emotional creative purpose of the French, lying between heroic and lyric opera: the love plot. For this purpose there were available a female vocal type of delicate yet passionate nature, and two male vocal types also essentially lyric in character. These three voices had to be explored for every possibility of sensitive treatment and for every color contained within a clearly defined scale of tone and movement, in order to produce varied dramatic combinations. With such a basis they could not become characters in an objective sense, but simply creatures of sex in various nuances of significance. What these basic conditions offer is not particularly the creation of the individual as such, but rather the opportunity to treat the relations between persons—the atmosphere they breathe, as exemplified in the strongest and most mysterious of these relations: love. This is passion not, as in Verdi, simply as a motivating factor; it is passion as the subject of the action.

This means that the figures themselves no longer stand out sharply against the horizon, as they do in Verdi. They are dissolved in a shimmering atmosphere in which they seem to flow together. Indeed, they become a part of the atmosphere. The element in which they have their being is their environment, the scent and sound of their surroundings made an integral factor in the behavior of human beings. The voice becomes the object of sensual desire or the medium through which such desire is expressed. The drama, limited to two male voices and one female voice, becomes a play of love and jealousy. The jealousy is between two lovers, or, at times, between one lover and one paternal or in some way supernatural accompanying figure.

These conditions are rooted as much in the cultural and spiritual as in the musical and vocal circumstances governing French opera. Out of them there develops, growing beyond the *comique,* the first really national French species, in a comprehensive sense: the lyric opera. It is so definitely national that, like the German operas of Weber, Marschner and Lortzing, or the Italian *buffa,* or the early works of Verdi, it does not permit of translation into foreign tongues or transplantation onto foreign stages without disfigurement and vulgarization. This is true even of those individual works that have become naturalized in foreign countries. There is something essential that simply cannot be transplanted: the spell of the language, the charm of the thought-structure based upon it, the special and characteristic externals connected with it, the inevitable marks of national temperament—all these things united in the sound of the voice. Climatically and physiologically conditioned, the voice can sound as it is intended to, and as the nature of the works demand, only when all these circumstances are properly related. There are works that grow beyond the language background from which they sprang. There are others so deeply dyed in the color of the language that gave them birth that they do not sound as they should if their relation to that language is broken. These are the truly national works. Every national culture has produced them. Their transplantation into other soils almost always leads to misunderstandings. This is what happened to French lyric opera, although some of its most important works have found a lively echo on the German stage.

This is true especially of the first great work of the species: Gounod's FAUST, or, as the revised German title reads, MARGARETHE. This is still not a pure example of lyric opera, to be sure. The scenic requirements, the large-scale ballet, the choral and ensemble writing, still show the urge towards grand opera. But the musical nature of Gounod and his choice of subjects made it a lyric opera, most closely related to the Verdi operas of the same period. The bass rôle of Mephisto is a vocal rarity. Kept for the most part to the higher, baritone register, Mephisto is a transitional character between Meyerbeer's sinister Bertram and the solitary masculine figures of Verdi. The other vocal types are lyric throughout. The high female voices are distributed among the sentimental soubrette, who is also a coloratura singer, in the title rôle; the soubrette in a man's rôle, especially popular on the French stage (Siebel), and the comic alto. Among the men's voices, it is the tenor, having only melody of soft outlines to sing, that dominates. Beside him stands the counter-figure, in this case animated by a brother's jealousy, of Valentine, the lyric baritone. With the bass, Mephisto, we thus have potentially the Mozartean sextet-grouping of the voices, as in FIGARO and DON GIOVANNI, although actually the grouping does not exceed the quartet. This is in the lyric center of the work, artistically its best realized portion—the second act—after which it gives way to trio groupings. The trio is really style-determining for this species, but in this work it is not achieved in the soprano-tenor-bass form until the end. Before that there is much surprising accessory material, which seems to embody a strange mixture of styles, although in the nature of its expression it remains within lyric bounds. The lyric character is determined by the plot as well, which is a love-story, containing some weird and supernatural elements but always related to the central love-theme. It makes use of figures descended through poetry from folk origins and thus presents the prototype of that moving delicacy in acting which is desired and intended in the lyric opera.

The connection of the subject with Goethe's poem

thus did no harm to Gounod's FAUST even in Germany. Rather, it enhanced its popularity, as it did that of Ambroise Thomas' MIGNON, which followed close upon Gounod's work. In MIGNON the lyric trio-opera type is already clearly defined. The relations to grand opera disappear. There is only a short ballet at the beginning of the first act. On the other hand, dialogue is interpolated again, with a certain melodramatic undercurrent. In the beginning there are two women's voices—the coloratura soubrette Philine and the lyric Mignon, kept for the most part within the darker middle register. But Philine, except at the beginning, is not an ensemble figure at all. She is entirely absent in the last act, where the action is shared by Mignon, the lyric tenor, and the lyric baritone, who appears as the father and rival. The vocal combination is already fixed in its salient features, and the male types are unchanged. Likewise unchanged remains the division of the women's voices into the coloratura higher register and the lyrically more sensitive medium register, which has the advantage of the natural vocal color of speech. The motivating force of these vocal resources is the simple love story, this time without the episodic accessory effects of FAUST, and limited exclusively to the touching accents of longing, desire, or renunciation.

All this is simply realized, as regards both language and melody. French lyric voices were not capable of extended singing, or of spinning out a tonal phrase to any great lengths, so that a song-like form, a melodic line of an essentially folk type, was a fundamental prerequisite. The declamatory accent is important, too, but it receives a simple, non-pathetic, yet melodically appealing guise. Clarity, acuteness, tenseness of expression are the basic qualities, applied to an elementary phenomenon of human emotion, represented by the desiring and desired woman between two men.

2

Such was the situation that Bizet found before him. He found, besides, the Verdi of AÏDA, and a Wagner not yet fully developed, but in the main already recognizable. In Rome, where he sojourned about the beginning of the sixties as holder of the *Prix de Rome,* he learned to know the Italian theatre thoroughly, and the Paris performance of TANNHÄUSER and all that followed it made it impossible for him to overlook Wagner. Meyerbeer's L'AFRICAINE, the jealousy opera in heroic style—another trio-opera employing soprano, tenor, and baritone—had not been produced until 1865. Nobody knew, of course, that Moussorgsky was creating his BORIS at this time, but in Paris FAUST and MIGNON had been followed by other works of the same composers, among which Gounod's ROMÉO ET JULIETTE had had exceptional success in France. It

GEORGES BIZET

was a period of unusual tension; yet, despite all conflicts, a time of greater inner certainty. For the outlook was much the same in all the musical countries; only the forms of realization showed how various were circumstances and resources. And now appeared the one great masterpiece of French lyric opera, surpassing every example that had preceded it: CARMEN.

That it was not immediately recognized, and that it later—fortunately for its effectiveness—received, instead of dialogue, recitatives from a hand other than that of the composer—these facts do not detract from the importance of the first appearance of CARMEN. For it is already the work in which all the basic characteristics of the lyric opera are brought to their highest development—free, unforced, produced solely by the kindling power of the subject. Once more this subject exhibits the characteristic idea of the lyric opera: love and jealousy in a triangle of one woman and two men, in simple and moving form, free of all sentimentality. This is love as a primitive force, possessed almost of the power of destiny in classic drama. A connected feature is the spell of a special environment, important for the dramatic purpose of the lyric opera. Through the combination of Spanish and gypsy coloring, CARMEN has an almost exotic charm, while the objectiveness of the action and its everyday nature create, through their apparent restraint and simple clarity, a counter-spell that enhances the tension.

The conventional elements, on the other hand, are slight, notably in that part of the first act where the action is set in motion. The four-act form made necessary a certain tension. The sentimental figure of Micaela, and the picturesque choruses, dances, and portrayal of *milieu,* creates a fullness of episodic detail that carries the action forward through the first three acts to a point from which such a landslide as occurs in the last act is possible. This last act is in every respect—as an artistic conception, as a dramatic contrasting of the voices, and as a revelation of their animal nature—the distilled content of the work. It is characteristic again that the climactic line leading to this fourth act was at first not recognized as such. The conventional first act was well received, but a flagging of enthusiasm led to the fiasco of the last act—confirmation of the fact that CARMEN marks the turning point in the conception of the nature of the lyric opera.

CARMEN is the basic type of the trio opera—not in its use of ensemble, but in the working-out of the acting characters. They are here conceived absolutely primitively—especially the woman. She has the Mignon mezzo tone-quality, associated in German ideas with the somewhat unctuous alto, but really to be taken only as the voluptuous low tone of the French female voice.

The physical demands made upon the voice are comparatively slight. The relation with language is basic. Every curve of the vocal line meets a requirement of the declamation. The latter is, so far as possible, related to dance and song form. The color of the voice is stressed, rather than its singing quality: in the card song, for example, the dark shades, in a heavy, dragging line; and, as a contrast, the dance rhythms, only sketchily clothed in tone, of the Seguidilla.

Similarly, every passage Carmen sings is a new mask, mirroring the man she is addressing. The receptive nature of woman is portrayed with uncanny realism in her change of tone as she addresses the passers-by, José, Zuniga, the smugglers, Escamillo. To each she is a different woman, changing the sound of her voice, the character of her melody, her mood, her tempo, and all within modest vocal limits. She is wholly herself only in the weary, scale-wise rise and fall of the melody of the card song, and in the dramatic arioso dialogue in the last act. The mimic significance of the voice, its true dramatic function and power of characterization, were never so strikingly displayed, and never with such subordination of all its singing qualities, in the ordinary sense; indeed the conception of woman as a primitive creature was never developed to such an extent out of the qualities of the voice itself. One recognizes the difference if one compares Carmen with the other female singing rôles of the work: Frasquita, Mercedes, Micaela. All these are singers, standing in clearly defined relations to the conventional vocal types. Carmen remains outside their circle. For that very reason, she is the completed realization of an elemental nature evolved out of the possibilities for dramatic characterization that belong to the voice.

The two men are determined by the nature of this central female figure. José, the French tenor who depends on the lightness of his high register and the appealing softness of his voice, is here whipped out of a state of passive endurance into live, human, passionate action by the inciting temperament of the woman. His vocal line ends in the cry of the animal, and the last big duet scene of the couple ends in spoken words—tones that have lost definite pitch.

The baritone is a less active figure. He is not an active force, but a simple fact. His song, based on an elementary march type of melody, is solely a sort of refrain that marks every turn in the action. He simply embodies the natural masculinity of the baritone as opposed to the exceptional sensitivity indicated by the tenor. The background characters are only sketched: the mocked lover, the bass Zuniga; the two smugglers, descended from the *buffo* type and intensified to the point of crafty seriousness; Mercedes and Frasquita. But the manner in which they are used to paint the environment lifts them out of the class of mere dramatic properties and makes them organic and living types.

Then there is a new type of ensemble. It is recruited no longer from among the principals, but from the ranks of the minor players. In the quintet, the chief ensemble of the whole work, only one of the principals takes part —Carmen. And even she is used at first only as a filling-in voice. The piece has no direct relation to the dramatic content of the work, nor is it, like similar pieces in Gounod or Verdi, a bringing together of the basic forces. From an external dramatic view it would seem to be only an effective interpolation. Its one important episode—Carmen's refusal to take part in the smuggling —could take place just as well outside this particular frame. This enclosing of a portion of the action corresponds to that of Carmen's card song in the women's trio of the third act. But the significance of the quintet in relation to the atmosphere and the psychological preparation for the events that follow, is so important that its absence is not conceivable without injury to the effect of the whole. It is precisely here that the special treatment of the voices, their hurried whispering, brings about the intensification of the sense of a ruling destiny that determines events. The chorus also serves this same purpose of making clear the environment in which the action takes place. This is extensively the case in the first act, where it is minutely subdivided so that children's, men's, and women's choruses form numerous individual groups: strollers, soldiers, girls from the cigarette factory. And these groups are never brought together into a combined chorus. Not until the conventional climax in the finale of the second act is there a combined chorus tone that really sounds like an operatic ensemble. The smugglers' choruses of the third act preserve this character in their underlying coloring; and then the march in the fourth act is reduced again to the introduction of singing supernumeraries. At this point the chorus has fulfilled its purpose as an instrument of tonal illumination. Now it is only a matter of individuals, and the mass disappears.

The orchestral treatment is especially subtle, and particularly the treatment of the woodwinds. Every form of mass treatment vanishes; or, when it does occasionally appear, as in Escamillo's scenes, it is immediately recognizable as an effect for the sake of contrast. This orchestra is not the active bearer of the harmony, nor is it subordinated to the singing voice. It is the light and air in which the characters of the action live and breathe. It is not intellectually reflective, but it is full of intuitions and sudden realizations. It is silent in the moments of greatest dramatic tension, limited to a few chords of recitative accompaniment, only to break out anew in support and intensification of the singing voice. The elements of harmony, of chamber music, and of color are equally represented, but limited and defined by the laws of the most intensely concentrated expression. It is just in this almost aphoristic concentration, in the avoidance of everything in the nature of flourishes or fine phrases, that the sturdy vigor and force of Bizet's orchestra consists. The effect of something not fully expressed, something only indicated in the flash of a sharp light, characterizes the entire impression. The single flute or trumpet is not a solo in the old sense. It is an abbreviation for a sound conceived as fuller than this, here represented only by its most characteristic color. Only within an orchestral tone so purified, so full and yet so transparent, could the French singing voice move freely and independently.

It seems exaggerated, of course to claim that all this, and with it the entire conception of everything that the CARMEN style means to the opera, was the result of taking a woman's voice as model, and of the urge to give it such expression, in speech and song, character and action, as would offer the most productive employment of its possibilities. But in view of the conditions that govern the creative process—conditions which have really nothing to do with purely rational considerations—the claim is justified. Only around such a concept as a center was it possible to construct a work that must, in its simple reality, display its national character in every fibre, to an extent never before reached by any

French work. Carmen's voice is, with all its advantages and all its limitations, the musically sensitive basic type of a nation. In its entirely individual tonal nature it is suited as no other to the expression of a mixture of melancholy and frivolity, sensuality and contempt for death. It is a sort of translation of Don Giovanni into feminine terms, filled with the same uncontrollable temperament as its prototype. Only recognition of this deepest impulse makes clear the nature of the whole opera. Only this recognition makes it understandable that such world-conquering and unique success should have been achieved by a work which, though certainly a conception of genius masterfully realized, is still in the narrow sense no isolated artistic creation.

Next after CARMEN, both in time and in success, follows LES CONTES D'HOFFMANN. Offenbach, who was almost twenty years Bizet's senior, helped to discover him (in a contest for a prize offered by Offenbach and won jointly by Bizet and Lecocq) and then outlived him by several years. Presumably he heard CARMEN performed, but he never heard his own single work in the field of lyric opera. LES CONTES D'HOFFMANN first appeared on the stage after Offenbach's death, in 1881, six years after CARMEN. Its course was similarly triumphal, although Offenbach's work is not filled with a force of such general significance and its sphere is therefore smaller. But within this sphere it exhibits the same law of illustration and characterization, the same division of forces and temperaments. What it lacks in animal spontaneity, as compared with CARMEN, it makes up in the delicate adjustment of its inner organism. The fundamental idea of basing the action on the voices is operative here too, and everything else remains, almost more clearly than in CARMEN, incidental. The chorus serves only as a frame: the work is unique in its treatment of the three middle acts as dreamlike tales, enclosed by the choral scenes, prologue and epilogue.

Connected with this scheme is the central dramaturgic idea of the changing voice of woman. Woman appears in three forms, each contained in one act, which together illustrate all the types that naturally belong to the lyric opera: the coloratura soubrette, the dramatic mezzo-soubrette, the lyric-sentimental soubrette. To the female voice completed in these three types corresponds the sensualist Faust-José type of tenor, representing man reduced to bondage, who remains the same in the face of all woman's metamorphoses. The other male figure, the baritone, is, on the contrary, changeable, in response to the changeableness of the eternal Eve. He is here conceived with a Mephistophelian exterior as guiding and profiting by the play of the sexes, as the demon who awakens desire and decrees separation, as the evil magician who casts the deluding spell of love. He is almost like the Verdi baritone types, except that he stands not, like Iago, entirely apart from women, but among them. He is the true giver of life and death, of fulfilment and disappointment.

This baritone figure, with its threefold mirroring of woman, is among the strangest creations of fancy. It received ever new stimuli from the continuous changes going on in its surroundings and thus escaped the necessity of unified treatment, for which Offenbach's powers would hardly have sufficed. A related phenomenon is the sort of half-light that pervades the whole work and gives it, in contrast to the tragic realism of CARMEN, the tint of tragi-comic fantasy. The idea of an enduring unity in the variety of the world of appearance, of continuous recurrence, and of the generic in the expressive life of the opera, was never so undisguisedly and naïvely exalted into a creative principle as in this work, which thus possesses a symbolic importance beyond its own particular significance.

It is striking that all the lyric operas are taken either directly or indirectly from literature: FAUST, MIGNON, WERTHER, are borrowed from Goethe; CARMEN is based on a short story of Mérimée; LES CONTES D'HOFFMANN is a sort of anthology around the figure of the tale-writer himself. The authors of these arrangements had judgment enough to realize how far their versions were from the originals. But they felt no qualms in the matter. The thought of comparison in a literary sense did not occur to them. Two requirements only were essential: first, a love plot centering about a woman between two men; second, an environment filled with special characteristics of mood or color calculated to interweave the triangular plot, as a fateful story of jealousy, with the outside world—to make men appear as the products of their environment. Massenet stressed this fatalistic connection in his MANON. This work, and to an even greater extent all his other works, belong so completely to the French sphere of expression that no translation is possible—at least without harm to their characteristic qualities. Beyond these limitations, which are linked with the tender and amorous eroticism of the works, the creative problem remains unchanged. But the plot of three characters tends rather to become one of two characters, soprano and tenor. The function of the baritone is shifted outside the center of the circle where he joins the intrigue. An important feature of Massenet's works, and of those of Saint-Saëns, is the increasing tendency towards long-spun song, and the consequent increasingly melodic character of the treatment of words and language. Song was pressed into ever more delicate gradations of feeling, because the singing abilities of the French voice could hold their own musically and tonally only through this increasing lyricism. This is one of the paths that leads to Debussy, far in other respects as Massenet's art was, through refinement lapsing into the conventional again, from any renewal.

3

The principle of the *opéra lyrique,* as French treatment revealed, was not especially susceptible of change. It was bound to lead soon from the realism of Bizet into a new artistic system of illusion, if it could not gain new intensity by strengthening the types at hand. But the French singing voice was not richly enough endowed to make that possible. The course of French opera was set, therefore, in the direction of increasing refinement of shades of feeling and ever firmer integration of all atmospheric elements. Thus it finally arrived with Debussy at a realm of ethereal delicacy which is at the opposite pole from Bizet's naïve directness and which considerably narrows the sphere of its external influence.

The impression made in Italy by the example set by CARMEN was quite different. Here there were no limitations of voice, or of temperament, or of dramatic urge. On the contrary, the voice was ever eager for more singing. The more strongly the passions were aroused, the more vital the singing temperament became, and the more vigorously the dramatic urge asserted itself. Such passion and naturalism as Bizet had shown were necessary and sought after in Italy. All the inherited elements of opera on the other hand—especially the long-drawn-out plot, progressing only slowly and laboriously—were felt to be a hindrance. The only essential thing was the combat among the three voices, as exemplified in the *lyrique* and as embodied by Verdi in OTELLO. Here, too, there was the one woman between two men, of whom the stronger was, to be sure, not a lover but a sinister figure for whom woman was only an object. But the artistic conception was the same in Italy as among the French. Verdi, to be sure, had scorned environment because in his works the passions were so strong as to rob other factors of importance. To his successors, environment became important as color. But they contented themselves with drawing its broad outlines. The development of the plot was a secondary matter, and not essential to the opera, which was once again to create its effect solely through the voice. This was possible as soon as natural passions were allowed to speak. The more directly these passions were taken from real life, the surer the effect was bound to be. Historical subjects required explanation, but actuality explained itself, and passion derived from it could not help being promptly understood.

Out of the artistic naturalism of Bizet and the realism of the later Verdi, arose the "veristic" opera. This opera is distinguished by the reduction of everything having to do with plot to the form of a one-act play, by the incorporation of the choruses into isolated, episodic effects, picturesque or descriptive of a situation, by the omission of all subsidiary material, and by concentration upon the three voices of the *opéra lyrique.* But these are now Italian voices. The stronger the passions aroused by the genuineness of the stage action, the greater the expansion of the voice. It breaks the bonds even of Verdi's realism; it strives to realize in tone the extreme limit of excited intensity. The course of the action is directed so that these peaks of intensity follow each other in the closest possible succession, each mounting higher than the last. In this effort every conceivable means is employed to take direct hold upon the hearer. He must be startled, moved by the action, must feel himself a part of it as of an experience that befalls him in the street. Even date and place of the incident are given; it is guaranteed to be true; the audience can check up on it in the newspaper. *Verismo* makes this possible. Its characters are simple, everyday people. The things that happen to them can happen to anyone, and consciousness of that fact makes the effect the more penetrating. Of decisive importance is the moulding of the characters out of the force of passion—the power, the dynamic richness, yet also the sensitive flexibility of the voices. Thus arise characters like Santuzza and Turridu to whom Alfio is a motivating complement, similar—though not similarly equipped as regards the rest of their environment—to Canio and Tonio. This origin of the characters in passion is the essence of the *lyrique,* seen from the point of view of OTELLO, and realized with intentional, and of course for these talents necessary, artlessness.

The absence of spiritual demands that characterized this style could not help showing itself soon in the lack of any power of expansion. The one-act form was at bottom not a sign of concentration but a makeshift necessitated by poverty of invention; the use of the vocal types was an elementary contrast of given patterns without any inner connection. Puccini is the only one of the young Italians who has, besides an inventive gift, a sense of the inner law governing action and song, a sense of form and structure, a sense of the significance of character as a force that reveals itself and grows only in expansion. Yet he is a decadent and concluding figure. It therefore lies beyond both his ability and his purpose to find new, individual types. But he was able to combine the available types for the purposes of his own form. Out of artistic mediation between Italian power and French sensibility Puccini brought forth a new Latin model. The influence of Wagner, too, can be traced, especially in his free treatment of harmony. This type of play is not international; it represents the Latin man of the world. It achieves general acceptance the sooner because it is not fettered by the recognition of any conventional requirements and bears unmistakably conversational traits.

Puccini at first takes over the characterization as well as the course of action of the *opéra lyrique;* indeed, in his second work, MANON LESCAUT, he is in direct contact with Massenet. He retains, with one exception, the diminutive, sentimental, soubrette female type. The baritone remains the jealous, the scorned, or the plotting lover. Never, not even in the grotesque faun's mask of Scarpia, is he comparable to the large-scale baritone figures of Verdi. The tenor, too, is confined essentially to the lyric field. Only Cavaradossi, in the moment of highest intensity, breaks through into the heroic character, but without maintaining it. The basis of the *lyrique* remains unchanged throughout, although colored and decorated in many ways by the vocal elements of the environment.

But those figures which in French opera were so delicate and transparent now become vocally almost too substantial. They are also pathologically touched up in order to lend to their vocal resources a new tonal nuance through the addition of the note of suffering. Mimi is consumptive; the picturesque element of Butterfly is her Japanese character. Only Tosca stands more or less unattached in space. Of all Puccini's figures she is the closest to Verdi's. She herself is a singer. As such, she needs no other coloring than that which the naturally passionate nature of an especially attractive artistic woman gives her. This lack of special color makes possible Puccini's most realistic and musically richest and ripest work. The fact that at the same time it cannot do without the torture chamber and the execution shows the limitation of this art—its need for naturalism conceived in the grossest terms. But Puccini does not remain content, like Mascagni and Leoncavallo, with such passing effects. Out of the emotional outcry of the voice grows a new type of melody—the broad cantilena. It is intensified by the orchestral harmony, color, and dynamics, tossed off with the casualness of virtuosity.

This cantilena, too, is based upon the subtle building of momentary emotional states out of nervous reactions, and follows the course of events with the greatest elasticity. It is the occasional complement of the singing voice; it is never pure melodic line. At most it becomes a direct reflex, the tonal mirror of the visible impression made by the action. It does not spring directly into words, but embodies spiritual gesture. It is atmosphere, perspective, background. The orchestra is ever-changing in its individual functions, but it always abides by the basic command never to obscure the voice. It remains the costume for the three great vocal types, which, for the last Italian opera-composers of the 19th century, represent life and the play of life as far as these can be represented by the singing voice.

Besides his three chief works—BOHÈME, TOSCA, and BUTTERFLY—and before the unfinished TURANDOT, Puccini wrote another *buffa,* intended to serve as one member of a trilogy: GIANNI SCHICCHI. This is a strange echo of FALSTAFF, with its baritone central figure and the arabesque-ensemble grouped about him—the final document of an ensemble *parlando* created purely out of speech, in which the melodious songs of the lover-pair sound almost like parodies of a dream of youth. This work shows Puccini's high artistry as exemplified in a theme freely chosen, apart from the conditions which his historical position imposed on him. SCHICCHI is timeless—like all timeless things, without any specific application—a pure play of fantasy.

Within his period, Puccini stands as the perfecter of lyric opera, in the form which resulted from its being penetrated by the elements of Italian song. If in the process he received certain stimuli from Verdi as his only real successor, his methods nevertheless differed from Verdi's in one respect. For Puccini, woman is always the creative center. She is not merely, like Carmen, the inciting force. She dominates the singing and the action to such an increasing extent that the male figures finally become mere scaffolding and their best function is to make a duet possible. In this respect, too, TOSCA apparently still follows a middle course, while BOHÈME develops variety out of its subject matter in the shape of episodic ensembles. But in these works, too, the vocal and melodic style is conditioned by the emotional life and vocal type of Woman. In this feminism are to be seen the great cultural relations that bring the theatre of Puccini closer to the French *lyrique* than to Verdi, who belongs to another world. At the same time, they establish a spiritual connection between French opera and the theatre of Richard Wagner.

4

In France, meantime, Wagner had become as thoroughly known and admired as the *opera* side of French taste permitted. The other side, interested not in the accents of pathos, in rhetoric, or in gesture, but in the sound-element of language, fought against the foreign element and its goal. It attempted to mobilize against them the natural song potentialities of the French language. The *lyrique* was a counter-phenomenon of this sort. But, unawares, it lacked the direct descent of vocal line from language-characteristics necessary to organic connection of speech and vocal character. The *lyrique* was always concerned with integration of the language element into the given formal structure of the music. It always respected the special laws governing the musical organism. These laws rested partly upon the periodic song, but chiefly upon the prevailing dance-like character of instrumental music. The feeling for these musical forms had so thoroughly permeated the consciousness of Western Europe, that it seemed impossible to create a form of song based purely upon language, without the same sort of periodic symmetry, harmonic and rhythmic.

But what was not possible to the Western European, even of revolutionary tendencies, was achieved in complete freedom—that is, under the sole law of necessity—by a Russian. Moussorgsky was not a professional musician and was therefore technically unhampered. He believed that song should arise not out of the symmetrically stylized instrumental music of Europe, but out of the laws of national languages. Thus he wrote, after many other attempts, his chief work, BORIS GODUNOFF. Here the declamatory setting of language was fundamental and creative. Moussorgsky, however, proceeds from the sentence structure, and not, like Wagner, from the individual word. From the sentence structure he builds a sort of recitative-like arioso. For this construction, to be sure, the simple and natural singable quality of the Russian language was a prerequisite. There is, in fact, no language except Italian that lends itself so readily to singing as Russian, and none that disposes of such rich material as Russian, particularly among men's voices. Moussorgsky found formal support for his style in Russian folk-song, and for his treatment of speech-melody and of harmony in Russian church music.

Thus there were several points of departure for a work of which the central figure is the strong and dominating character of the baritone. But here the baritone bears no exceptional psychological relation to the separate phenomena of the outer world. He is really the center, the essence of the creative idea, whose force radiates from him in various directions towards the women's and particularly towards the men's ensembles. The counter-force is the chorus, for which Moussorgsky again found precedent in Russian folk-music. Thus this drama is based solely upon the counterplay between the chorus action, treated with the greatest variety and movement, and the heroic criminal figure of Boris. The love-plot of the *lyrique* is narrowed down to an episodic intrigue of consciously conventional style—the so-called Polish act. The tenor figure of the false Dimitri, apparently a counter-figure to Boris, really remains on the periphery of the action, a mere auxiliary to its development, and gradually disappears. As the one counter-rôle, the pure bass figure of the monk-evangelist Pimen provides the introduction and conclusion which serve as a historical frame to the story.

This curious work, which does not belong to the normal course of history, was produced as early as 1874 (that is, a year before CARMEN) in St. Petersburg. It became known in Western Europe only several decades later, earliest in France, and latest—forty years after the first performance—in Germany. New to Western Europe were the charm of Eastern melody and the exotic fullness of the harmony, as well as the treatment of the relation of speech and melody—apparently primitive, yet subject to deep-lying laws. Here was a way to give voice and speech a clear path. It permitted song to grow out of speech and yet to sing out freely, and at the same time to refine itself beyond the sphere of the spoken word without placing any intellectual burden upon sounding tone.

This, after the preparatory clearing done by Massenet, was the path taken by Debussy—the most original of French composers since Bizet. Debussy is, in fact, a counter-figure to Bizet. He is the personification of that pure Gallic-Latin nature which in its inclination towards ethereal delicacy and emotional restraint belongs to the soil and climate of France. Debussy took his ground-plan from the *lyrique;* the three-character play of jealousy between two men competing for the love of one woman. But the more the spirit and poetic tendency of the language determined the musical course of events, the more the outlines of the characters were bound to melt away and outer occurrences to be stripped of reality and crowded into a sort of external symbolic series of events. All the more reason why individual characterization as an end in itself should disappear. Only the life of the figures in relation to one another

CLAUDE ACHILLE DEBUSSY

could be the object of representation. Language counted no longer as a means of holding things together and sharpening the emotions, but as a means of inner clarification. Music had to carry forward this process of spiritual illumination by further enhancing the increasingly ethereal qualities of language.

Maeterlinck's PELLÉAS ET MÉLISANDE offered Debussy the appropriate literary foundation: a last fine play of love, love that hardly touches with desire the person of the beloved woman, that merely strokes her hair, yet without a word takes such deep possession of her soul that in reality the wildest sensuality seems unimportant as compared with this union of souls veiled in the most delicate agitation. Events take place as if at the bottom of the sea, invisible, afar off, with a sort of inhuman pitilessness. But the visible surfaces of the music, moved deep within itself by these events, show only slight reflections. In this way Debussy's opera is the model of French musico-dramatic production. For here the voices sing what is really suited to their abilities. They move in a sphere of purely lyric expression from which all traces of other types of material have vanished. The lyricism of the soft female voice, very flexible and fine but not at all strong, is brought back in the chanting songs of Mélisande to its basic dimensions. Thus it produces the most beautiful and sublime tones of which the French female voice is capable. The essence of the masculine voice, here so variously assorted in range, is similarly brought to its highest development in the unconsciously desiring and joyous tones of the deeper register of the tenor voice of Pelléas, and in the tones of Golaud, who though tormented with pain and uncertainty yet keeps a dogged hold on what is rightfully his. The Pimen-like bass figure of the King, Arkel, completes the list of principal characters.

Undoubtedly there are links between this story and that of TRISTAN UND ISOLDE, just as Debussy's music, despite its conscious originality, is full of Wagner, especially of PARSIFAL. These are the symptoms of the deep spiritual relations between the two men. To try to shut one's eyes to those relations would be purposeless; on the other hand, their presence and the recognition of them does not affect an estimate of Debussy's spiritual independence. The tie that binds him to Wagner is one of opposition. It is no less important on that account than the tie that binds him to Moussorgsky, which is combined with his attempt to go back beyond Gluck to the early, national art of Rameau. It is back to Rameau, too, that Debussy's relation of special harmonic functions leads. He does not employ the chorus of Moussorgsky. He dissolves it, to a certain extent, in a harmonic style that intensifies to the utmost the sublimation of word and spiritual gesture, the process of spiritual rarefaction. His orchestra, too, is the opposite of the Wagner orchestra, which explains and makes psychological comment on what is happening. Debussy's orchestra completely achieves its characteristic French function of providing in the harmony the atmosphere in which the voice has its being. His harmony, made up of novel, strange, oriental, and mediaeval chords, creates a shimmering atmosphere of reverberating and merging tones that mirrors what seems by comparison to be the earthbound explicitness of word-sounds in song. But beyond this contrast in orchestral point of view, the means employed in modern French harmony are often strikingly similar to those in Wagner's harmony. Here too, then, above individual spiritual differences is manifest an organic material connection between the products of different times.

PELLÉAS appeared in 1902, two years later than TOSCA and the LOUISE of Charpentier. This latter work is also typically Gallic. The central figure is a Carmen in Parisian terms, a tamed, middle-class Carmen; her lover and her father are accompanying figures, thoroughly successful so far as the conception of the types is concerned, but too local in color, and lacking in strong, expansive force. Dukas's ARIANE ET BARBE-BLEUE, more earthy in its musical conception than Debussy's PELLÉAS, does not achieve the representative significance of that unique and inimitable work. With Dukas's opera a great era of spiritual independence comes to an end for French opera, just as Italian romantic opera reaches its conclusion in Puccini—a figure much more influential externally than Dukas, but of similar artistic significance. Both developments end in the type characteristic of the lyric opera with its pronounced three-character plot, with jealousy as the motivating force, and with the decisive significance of the *milieu* as a determining influence upon the plot. Characters of an unusual sort are lacking, as are any problems outside or above man. Relations spin themselves like invisible threads. They draw nourishment out of the air and the persons who seem to act are only sails to catch the wind, only means of utterance. These relations always circle about the theme of the struggle of two men for a woman. Santuzza alone excepted, woman is always the desired one, and the plot consists in making her appear ever more desirable and more difficult of attainment. This brings about the tension and the ever further unfolding of the voices. They are continually striving for the heights of emotion. It is emotion that animates the form as well, and thus the connection with naturalism is preserved. Debussy's art is an exception, a flight into domains ever further from reality; it is to some extent a conscious reaction against this highly emotional naturalism.

With Dukas and Puccini, the last creative aftermath of the work of Verdi, Bizet, and Moussorgsky had made its appearance. What the Latin spirit deemed adaptable from the work of Wagner had also been taken over. Italian and French opera—and Slavic opera, which is related to both—had reached a point beyond which only repetition and no further productive development was possible. A new and individual species had run its course, with all the metamorphoses that the interplay of the most varied forces of the time could bring about. A new sphere of creative activity, arising from the nature of the Latin voice, had been outlined and fulfilled. It had established the productiveness of a changed behavior of the singing voice according to new laws, and it now ended where it began.

Chapter XI

HISTORICAL OPERA

Strauss Pfitzner d'Albert Schreker
Busoni Strawinsky Post-War Opera

I

IN the first decade of the new century the creating of opera begins to disappear outside Germany.

With Debussy vanishes the last great representative of the Gallic side of Latin Art. His contemporaries—Dukas, Charpentier, Ravel—who survive him, achieve nothing but scattered individual works. The younger generation produces no successors. Opera ceases to tempt creators; instrumental chamber combinations and small experimental forms reign supreme. The picture in Italy is similar. Puccini's main work is completed with BUTTERFLY in 1904. Of his one-act operas, only GIANNI SCHICCHI is important. TURANDOT, not completed by the composer, represents a tapering off and not a new variation. There are, to be sure, a few cultivated and gifted men, like the lyrically very talented

Alfano, and Pedrollo, and Giordano; but none of them is able to step outside the circle already described for them.

The Slavic people bring even less that is new. Smetana's Bartered Bride, composed in 1866, remains, with a few other works of this master, the foundation for Czech activity. Dvořák's operas are not important. In Russia, Moussorgsky's Boris is an isolated work. Musicians of talent try the application of Russian motives to the model offered by the *lyrique*. Here, especially in Tschaikowsky, there are many prophetic relations to Puccini. More important than the opera, for Russia, is the ballet. It grows out of French tradition, a new art-species of musical and physical expression, thanks to the extraordinary mimic and rhythmic gifts of the Russian in dance-pantomime. Once before, this art had served as the basis of the *opéra*. Now it brings forth upon the stage a new, ironic, parodistic type of musical fantasy-play. In this field unfolds the most original stage talent of the new century: Igor Strawinsky. But, just as happened in the case of Moussorgsky, it is a long time before Strawinsky becomes known in Western Europe. And even then, proper means are lacking to show the peculiar nature of his art. His dance-plays, calculated for visual illustration, must be content with abstract performances as orchestra suites.

In the rest of Europe an increasing lethargy spreads

over opera-production—except in Germany. Here a genuine creative fever breaks out. Two little-known works, DER BARBIER VON BAGDAD of Peter Cornelius and Hermann Götz's DER WIDERSPÄNSTIGEN ZÄHMUNG (THE TAMING OF THE SHREW), had survived from the Wagner period, and later received a literary and historical aura. To these were added, as direct descendants of Wagner, Hugo Wolf's CORREGIDOR, Humperdinck's HÄNSEL UND GRETEL, GUNTRAM, by Richard Strauss, KAIN, by d'Albert, DER ARME HEINRICH, by Pfitzner. From these works of the century's end the line veers towards Italy in d'Albert's TIEFLAND. Then come Strauss's series of great tone-poems for stage and orchestra: FEUERSNOT, SALOME, and ELEKTRA, and after these, the studies in archaic style: ROSENKAVALIER and ARIADNE. In among these come Pfitzner's ROSE, Busoni's TURANDOT and DIE BRAUTWAHL, Schönberg's ERWARTUNG and DIE GLÜCKLICHE HAND, Schreker's DER FERNE KLANG and, as regards date of composition, Strawinsky's PÉTROUCHKA. The dance continues with Pfitzner's PALESTRINA, Busoni's ARLECCHINO, and d'Albert's DIE TOTEN AUGEN. L'HISTOIRE DU SOLDAT, Schreker's DIE GEZEICHNETEN and DIE SCHATZGRÄBER, and Strauss's DIE FRAU OHNE SCHATTEN mark the end of the war period.

Now a new generation makes its appearance. Hindemith's one-act operas CARDILLAC and NEUES VOM TAGE, Krenek's ZWINGBURG, ORPHEUS, JONNY, Berg's Woz-

ZECK, and finally Weill's DREIGROSCHENOPER, MAHAGONNY, DER JASAGER, and DIE BÜRGSCHAFT, represent German post-war youth. With them ranks the French Milhaud with his CHRISTOPHE COLOMBE, while the Italians, Casella, Malipiero, and Castelnuovo-Tedesco, occupy themselves with opera on a smaller scale as artistic entertainment. Among these new products of the young generation, whose popularity, considerable at first, is beginning to wane, have come further large works of the older men: Strauss's INTERMEZZO and DIE ÆGYPTISCHE HELENA, Pfitzner's HERZ, Schreker's SCHMIED, Strawinsky's ŒDIPUS. In these works, too, an unmistakable slackening of effect—indeed, of creative forces themselves—is evident. About the turn of the third decade, creative activity is almost entirely choked off.

This series, whose outlines are here hinted at through its most important members only, at first makes the impression of an almost convulsive eruption, which in its precipitancy reveals no community of spiritual impulse behind its varied manifestations—in fact hardly permits of any organized approach to its consideration. It is to be observed that the greatest variety of styles is represented, not only in inspiration for conception and execution, but also in possibilities for practical performance. Since opera composition, while it still went on, had no satisfactory success, practical needs made increasingly necessary the systematic cultivation of the products of earlier periods of creative activity. But where were singers and performers to be found for these older works, which could be understood, and so re-created, only under definite conditions of period and style?

This was the beginning of a historically-minded, backward-looking age. With its creative activity, the question of reproduction was—as always in such a time—indissolubly connected. This became a problem because of the variety of demands it called forth. There might be either free, creative remodeling, or else purely imitative reproduction. Neither possibility admits of a really pure solution. The essence of artistic experience would really require that in all the representative arts new works should be continually created for contemporary use, and everything past should remain past, to be exhibited, if at all, only as a document of the past. All great creative periods have taken this stand. But no such strict solution of the problem of inheritance here comes into consideration. The two facts we have to consider are the still vital effect of inherited works, and the lack of sufficient opera-production in our own time. Both facts characterize the historically-minded age and the tasks assigned to it.

The problematic element in these tasks lies in the fact that this age lacks any direct relation of its own to the singing organ. Other elements, too, have arisen—

elements of an orchestral, that is, a reflective and speculative, nature; considerations of subject matter; ideologies having to do with drama or philosophy; with everything, in fact, except song. Opera is viewed more and more as a play which more or less incidentally makes use of song and music. Style-determining laws evolved from the raw material of opera have fallen so completely into oblivion that finally they cease to be believed in at all. They are considered at best curiosities of a long-forgotten time, no longer to be taken seriously. A historical and scientific view of music takes the place of a creative use of tone. Music changes from a thing of sounding tones to a picture made up of notes in black and white.

The consequences of this development, as far as creation is concerned, are the need and desire to imitate one style or another, without true understanding of its creative foundation. Voices are used, now in one style of characterization, now in another. The operatic scheme is based upon the externals of characterization, without any realization of its inner functional sense. Plots become expressions of ethical, social, and religious convictions. There is no understanding of the fact that the nature of the opera plot is never primary, as is that of the drama plot, but always the product of a creative vocal conception out of which the human figure grows. This lack of understanding of the vocal basis of opera is magnified by a general predilection for instrumental effect. Yet even here the inner vocal treatment takes form out of the never quite suppressible vitality of the material, at least so far as it is not overpowered by other, speculative elements.

Out of this situation, which rests upon the creative desires of mere talents, and has no organic relation to the creative essence of the opera species, arise two types of composition: the symphonic opera, imitating Wagner, and the song-opera, imitating the Latin type based upon Puccini. The first species finds its most important representatives in Humperdinck, Pfitzner, and Strauss; the latter in d'Albert and Schreker. To these is added a third type, the most original of the three—the opera without song. This form arises primarily out of embarrassment, which, however, may be cleverly turned into a fruitful attitude, as in Strawinsky's pantomime. These are the three chief paths of post-war opera.

2

The model for the diversion of the creative impulse into symphonic instrumental channels was Richard Wagner. The strongest and most important all-around musical nature after him is Richard Strauss. The period of Strauss's creative activity is longer than that of anyone else since Wagner. It combines contrasted types in organic and logical relation, and includes in SALOME and ROSENKAVALIER two worldwide successes. Strauss's entire achievement, taken together, is a series of style experiments, feeling its way from one model to the next, surprisingly successful at two points, but permitting of no continuation along a straight line in the direction marked by the successful works, and always calling forth further experiment.

This shows Strauss's inner uncertainty concerning his relation to opera as a species. He begins, in GUNTRAM, with an imitation of Wagner. The origin of his symphonic orchestra is unmistakable, as is his dependence upon his prototype. Even the union of composer and librettist in one is imitated. GUNTRAM is so obviously connected with Wagner that one's only impression of the work is that it announces a new talent. From this point on, Strauss veers towards the path that really suits his nature, towards "tone-poems," as he calls his orchestral works. This designation of their spiritual and artistic structure is accurate. Strauss's programs are not merely emotionally related to symphonic form, they are organically interwoven with it. They deal, not like Liszt's, with confession or meditation, but primarily with plot, musical history in harmonic, instrumental motion, just as do Wagner's works. But Strauss's program at first does not extend into vocal and scenic spheres of expression; it remains confined to the realm of the instrumental.

Only after far-reaching exploitation of this instrumental realm does further expansion occur towards words, towards visible scenery, towards the singing voice. Now, however, the voice does not lead. It is the final climax and translation of the primarily instrumental action, out of which it grows, and it acts as programmatic guide where pure instrumental expression fails to be definite, or where realms of expression are entered which cannot be reached by any instrument. Even in these cases the vocal tone is significant only as color and as part of the harmony.

Thus does Wagner's conception of the union of word and tone finally fall apart. The word, as such, serves now for programmatic explanation. The voice becomes a part of the orchestra, supported by it, receiving its activating impulses from it, fulfilling its function as a singing instrument of the orchestra while the explanatory word is added by a cultivated man of letters, in a form independent of tone. The old, pre-Wagner conception of the text reappears, in inverted form: it is no longer, as it once was, a basis for the music; it is now an ingeniously assimilated explanation. The tonal march of events goes on in the orchestra; the singing voice merely joins it as the final tonal climax. The orchestra, once the bearer of absolute, abstract ideas, turns, impelled by the urge to greater intensity, to that field of expression to which lyric opera, in a different way, owes its character: to the eroticism of the play of the sexes.

Thus there grow out of the symphonic tone-poem the symphonically based vocal and scenic stage-pieces: FEUERSNOT, SALOME, and ELEKTRA. The sexual act itself is their subject matter. It forms the goal of creative fancy expressed with naïve symbolism in FEUERSNOT and from then on intensified by the ever stronger intermingling of pathological elements. Strauss thus arrives in his vocal characterization at clear dependence upon the lyric opera of the Latins, especially in the conception of the leading female voice. This dramatic type—beginning with Diemut, and including Salome and Elektra—stands between the sexes, much like the type formed by Puccini in his best-realized female figure, Tosca. Opposite this figure, and at first seeming to occupy a central position, is the baritone: Kunrad, Jochanaan, Orestes. The tenor loses his lover's rôle and becomes a character part: Herod, Ægisthus.

In this change in the nature of the tenor, an important change for the entire future of opera is predicted: a turning away from the use of voices as reflecting primarily erotic sound-impulses. This statement may seem surprising when applied to the field of expression of a Richard Strauss, especially in view of works like SALOME and ELEKTRA. But while the process is with him only a subsidiary phenomenon, recognizable only in so far as the impulses of the main action are not at work, it is symptomatic. The tenor as lover disappears, changing into a character part, hysterical, pathological, almost possessed. This change takes from the female voice a motivating element, a result that was bound to make itself felt the moment emphasis on the orchestra diminished, and the natural force of action of the voices came to the fore again.

This conception of the tenor tone as an abnormal character color is not new. Mozart's Basilio is perhaps the stem from which the entire line of such figures sprang; Halévy's fanatic Eléazar belongs to it; Wagner's Loge and Mime and Moussorgsky's Idiot continue it. All these show the transformation of the tenor from the lover to the degenerate, the deformed, the outcast. The sound of the tenor voice arouses thoughts no longer of tenderness but of the singular and the grotesque.

This form of tenor characterization is an early sign of a newly reawakening sense of the individual significance of the voice. Strauss's course after ELEKTRA shows with increasing force the extraordinary reaction of the voice on all who concern themselves with it. It causes the most confirmed skeptic in the end to recognize vocal values. Strauss completed with ELEKTRA the composition of symphonic opera with all its magic of color and harmony. In proportion as he had thoroughly explored this field, in his realm of expression, he found the mystery of the singing voice increasingly attractive. Strauss is another to think of the singing voice chiefly as female. The male becomes for him more and more the representative of the species, with the naïvely explicit aim of enjoyment. The orchestra remains an important factor in the action but loses its leading position. As soon as the voice is heard as really singing, the symphonic function of the orchestra at once diminishes.

Thus arises one of the most delightful style-works of an epigonic era: DER ROSENKAVALIER, a story of three women's voices hovering about the bass figure of a manikin sort of man—clumsy, yet adroit enough—carrying on their interplay with one another, as with him, in the most varied ensemble combinations, finally breaking out in a trio that grows gloriously out of the voices themselves, and in a duet of fabulous delicacy and tonal beauty. This is, and deserves to be, Strauss's most living stage work next to SALOME, and like SALOME, moreover, a document of high musical genius. The voices—in the latter opera those of Salome and Herod, in ROSENKAVALIER those of the three women and Ochs—have achieved a physical existence independent of all instrumental or other purposes. What they sing and how they sing is not new in the sense of epoch-making creativeness. But it is a combination of a fully matured and now backward-looking orchestral and harmonic art with a renewed recognition of the ancient culture of voice and song.

The vision of this ancient culture, and a longing for it, hold Strauss the musician captive from this point on. He feels the great productive law even if it does not directly fit his musical world. So, in an art based on archaic styles, he seeks a middle path. The voice does not sing out freely, but it appears to do so, although it is bound up with the orchestral harmony and its melodic outline remains determined by instrumental considerations. Thus comes into being the magic score of ARIADNE. Further removed from life than ROSENKAVALIER, full of self-consciously aesthetic elements, it nevertheless maintains the equilibrium between the two style-determining factors—voice and orchestra. Thus comes, finally, DIE FRAU OHNE SCHATTEN—an attempt to develop both principles simultaneously and jointly, to re-inflate the orchestra, to carry it over from the symphonic into the *concertante* style, and at the same time to let the voices sing freely.

The attempt is too consciously and artificially made to result in anything organic, without any inner connection of its constituent elements. There follows, in INTERMEZZO, the especially curious attempt, indeed the most curious attempt among all Strauss's many activities, to evolve a new style of speech-song. The orchestra is retained as an important factor, as the vehicle of the melody, and the voice declaims along with it in realistic fashion and at times in set aria forms. For the first time since Wagner, the original relation between song and speech—the speech origin of song—is at least theoretically acknowledged: Strauss himself writes the text. But the inner restriction upon the orchestra does not permit his intuition to ripen into musically satisfying achievement. The voices mostly speak a kind of recitative, with little arioso interludes and a broadly conceived final duet, while the orchestra makes complementary music.

INTERMEZZO is Strauss's last style experiment. From here on, his road is lost in artistic reflections of a speculative nature. Even when he reduces the size of the orchestra, the works do not lose their instrumental-harmonic basis, for the fundamental concept has been formed and does not change. Thus his works taken as a body show reawakened interest in and love for the true value of the voice as the most important element in the opera; but they stop short of making that value the basis for a new creative point of view. The ties that bind even the most richly endowed musician of the time to the immediate past are too strong, the domination of basically instrumental-harmonic feeling is too powerful, while any conscious desire to effect a new creative approach on the basis of the voice is lacking. There is only a shrewd recognition, a literary relating to older styles, and an increasingly masterful treatment, of the vocal apparatus, on the basis of an unchangingly instrumental conception.

3

Strauss's origin and natural gifts indicated for him a road that led forth not, to be sure, from the primary material of the voice, but nevertheless from a generally musical beginning. He did not leave the ground of actual tone and of its laws, although his creative impulse turned from vocal to instrumental tone. But beside Strauss's attitude, another became current. It found Strauss's point of view too materialistic, licentious in its development, perverse in its subjects. Rejecting creation out of tonal material, it evolved an intellectual dramaturgy based chiefly on the work of Wagner, but in details also on that of Weber and Marschner. External construction, the general effect of the action, the modeling of the characters—everything, in short, really secondary, was now intellectually treated as primary.

Thus arose an aesthetic theory of "musical drama," which exalted Wagner's form to the realms of philosophic law. Opera acquired a metaphysical perspective and depended upon extratonal, intellectual matters for its effect. The chief cause for this apparent transfiguration is at first—in contrast to the case of Strauss—the anemia and general weakness of creative talents. They themselves lived and breathed the air of theorem rather than of sound. In addition, there was the general misunderstanding of the nature of the voice, and the sterility of attitudes which, once separated from their most natural creative core, became more and more lost in the depths of speculation. Thus opera, the simplest and most sensuous species of theatre-piece, became a medium of expression for extra-musical forces, which sought to make it over into an art positively cabalistic in meaning.

The initial work of this series is HÄNSEL UND GRETEL. Here, despite adroit handling, a contrast remains between a child-like, legendary, folk type of plot and the Wagner orchestra—somewhat overloaded as regards sound, harmony, and instrumentation. The vocal part is significant only in that the use of the female voice springs from the preference for simple song-forms. The example set by Humperdinck's treatment of the orchestra—combination of simple song-melody with an appearance of artistic polyphony and harmonic logic—proved handy for German composers of household-music, and was exploited in a rich practical literature of genre-pieces, idylls, comic or light operas in small forms.

In the work of Hans Pfitzner this type achieved an extension in size. Pfitzner became practically and theoretically the chief representative of this intellectual conception of musical drama. The unmistakable stamp of

Wagner's work is evident from DER ARME HEINRICH to PALESTRINA. But the special nature of its origin and artistic structure is ignored. It is taken as a norm, yet conceived and re-created with such fanatical ardor as to bring about an extraordinarily heightened receptivity, which, to be sure, remains unavoidably bound up with a corresponding narrowing of the spiritual sphere. This process of contraction, too, is a result of the drying up of creative sources, a product of artificial construction which aims at achieving out of opera the illusory picture of a musical drama, and so leaves out of consideration the basic element—the voice itself in its organic logic as well as in its possibilities of aesthetic effect.

The effect of the subject matter upon the creative work is to be seen in Pfitzner as in Strauss. But over and above all speculative tendencies there is always a subconscious striving for further modeling of the voices with the purpose of a new characterization and a correspondingly new conscious attitude towards the dramatic idea. In Pfitzner, as in Strauss, the treatment of the tenor is characteristic. In the two early works, DER ARME HEINRICH and DIE ROSE, he remains, like the works themselves, within the economical, almost ascetic scheme of Wagnerian abstraction. In the title rôle of PALESTRINA, however, a change is effected. This voice is deprived of any relation to woman. It remains confined to the expression of suffering, action, creative ecstasy—

in general, somewhat hysterical but pure virility. The need for complement in the female voice disappears, being represented here only in a sort of transfigured sensuousness reminiscent of Offenbach's CONTES D'HOFFMANN, in the picture of Lucrezia and in the singing angels. The female voice in this opera is, in fact, suppressed from every point of view, and in the action itself, in the male rôles sung by women—Silla and Ighino—its sphere is very limited. The action is fulfilled between the tenor and the heroic baritone as representatives of truly active power.

PALESTRINA is an opera of two men, which in the second act, at the complete disappearance of the leading tenor, is dissolved in a lively men's ensemble. Therewith a peculiarly modern current is imparted to this consciously backward-looking work, showing the force of the undercurrents and creative purpose of the time. PALESTRINA is one of the first operas in which the dawning goal of freedom from the erotic appears—or, in musical terms, in which the vocal treatment rests upon the juxtaposition of two male-voice types, taking over the central position and significance which female voices had hitherto possessed. In accordance with this new combination of vocal types, the orchestra, while it does not altogether lose its leading position, is nevertheless considerably restricted.

All this seems, indeed, the work rather of accident

than of purpose. Pfitzner's next opera, DAS HERZ, brings back the predominance of the romantic baritone, and as the most important female voice the figure of the boy Wendelin. This work is for several reasons not really typical. PALESTRINA remains the characteristic document of Pfitzner's art. It shows Pfitzner's awakening urge, like that of Strauss, to song and the voice. In Strauss this urge originates from musical considerations; in Pfitzner, from instinctive dramatic impulses. But in neither does it really break through. It is impeded in Strauss by his instrumental and harmonic tendency, and in Pfitzner by his basic intellectual attitude. In the former it ends up in the music-making of actors, and in the latter in doctrinaire theorizing and fantastic opera expressive of a basic philosophy. Pfitzner's work is denied any great, lasting success because, in contrast to Strauss's, it is not a free and natural manifestation of power, but a cramp of the spirit, caused by a lack of really productive substance.

4

Imitation of Wagner reigns in Pfitzner as in Strauss, whether it is concerned with the further development of the orchestral action or with intellectual propaganda. Forming a third group, two composers now appear who, also proceeding from Wagner as a starting point, very soon give evidence of an especially fine ear for vocal effect. In their conscious application of this subtlety to opera, they achieve an approach to the romantic opera, a connection between Wagner and Puccini. These men are Eugen d'Albert and Franz Schreker. D'Albert, born in the same year as Strauss, begins as a Wagner-imitator. With DIE ABREISE he goes over to the neo-Biedermeier style of Humperdinck. His most personal work is achieved in TIEFLAND, produced in 1903—three years after TOSCA. This is the lyric opera of romantic origin in its purest form. The three voices seem modeled directly after TOSCA; but they are more earthbound, have more animal strength, are more peasant-like and closer to the village environment that is exploited in the action and in the music with similar effect. Out of this successful variation, together with an adroit use of the voices, came a work of exceptionally widespread popularity. The essential nature of the opera had once again been captured, not by an original creative force, but in so powerful a repetition of basic characterization that the effect followed inevitably. This, it is true, was the height of d'Albert's achievement. Of his numerous later attempts to develop further in this direction only DIE TOTEN AUGEN, shot through with religious mysticism, made any important impression, though not even this work approached the popularity of TIEFLAND.

A figure of higher aspirations than d'Albert, who simply made music for the public, was Franz Schreker.

He, too, takes over the vocal grouping of the lyric opera. But he surrounds the three chief voices at first with an ensemble of solo voices and chorus which has marked individuality, and he develops this ensemble to a point of ecstatic intensity. A related achievement is his refinement of orchestral tone until it has an almost French atmosphere. With this there is the fantastic nature of the stage action, dissolving the definiteness of meaning of the French and Italian opera in an aura of symbolism.

Schreker belongs to the generation after Strauss, d'Albert, and Pfitzner. When he started out, the entire work of Puccini, together with PELLÉAS, LOUISE, TIEFLAND, lay already ten years behind, and Strauss had already arrived at ROSENKAVALIER. In Schreker the penetration of these influences is completed. The fact that the voices are led back from declamation influenced largely by literary and linguistic values to a really melodic language of song, shows the urge towards a new type of opera—produced with the means and the ideas of the old. As in Strauss, erotic experience is the center of the action. It is adapted to the vocal types available in French and Italian opera. Out of harmonic variety and vocal necessity the dramatic illusion takes tonal form. Thus the element of sound again takes first place, although from a point of view that does not make possible any new development. In Schreker as in d'Albert—and, in another form, in Strauss—the female voice remains in control. This condition determines the intellectual and musical tone of the whole, and testifies to the impossibility of further creative development. The same is true of Schönberg's two mono-dramas, which are to be regarded chiefly as fantasy-studies. In DIE ERWARTUNG as in DIE GLÜCKLICHE HAND, only one voice is active, and in VON HEUTE BIS MORGEN a quartet. But the voices simply explain things in words; the main action remains reserved to the orchestra. Thus the voice is here in even greater subordination than in Strauss, a mere aid and interpreter of the purely instrumental and harmonic intention.

5

Only one figure of this generation, Busoni, the German-Italian, proceeds from a realization of the opera's need for thorough remodeling. True, his stage works—TURANDOT, DIE BRAUTWAHL, ARLECCHINO, DOKTOR FAUST—are not completely without women. But in them the female voice, with the exception of the Enigma Princess Turandot, is only episodically used, and is thus consciously deprived of style-determining significance. To accomplish this it was not sufficient simply to write operas without love stories, for a change. The task consisted in achieving, through the special conditions governing and effects resulting from an opera of men, a new aim for opera as an art work, and thus to open a new road for operatic development. Eternal and deeply rooted in nature as is the theme of love between man and woman, and many as had been the metamorphoses through which it had passed since Mozart—its fertility for the purposes of an art-form tied to outward appearance was bound to diminish proportionally as its treatment became increasingly stereotyped. The love-story is one of the possibilities, not necessities, of opera. It had appropriated exclusive validity unto itself. It was now necessary for the basic purpose of opera to be made productive once more through creative remodeling.

That was essentially the purpose as well as the practical result of Busoni's great stimulating activity: the liberation of opera from the sphere of love-plots, and the achievement of a new sphere of action above and beyond the circle of erotic fantasy.

Thus Busoni arrived at a vocal characterization which is primarily non-erotic. The characters so produced lead into a new, immaterial world of new contrasts, new movements, new paths of thought. It was not sufficient to write new parts for the tenor; Strauss and Pfitzner had done that too, and even stressed its characteristic nature. But Busoni's tenors are of another sort, from head to toe. Thusmann, the involuntary hero of DIE BRAUTWAHL, and Mephisto are sparks of a new and lighthearted irony—of *serenità.* No matter whether in a tragic or a humorous direction, this quality gives the piece a spiritual middle course, thus determining its attitude, its style, its manner of performance, its whole tone, just as the dramatic female voice does in Wagner, or the baritone in Verdi. Busoni's operas are tenor operas. The sound of the tenor voice, conceived in glassy, transparent form, above sex, gives these works their individual stamp. It penetrates the tone-world of the opera through and through, and gives transparency to its massive form.

Thus the Busoni tenor operates as the tonally determining and motivating element upon which all other factors are based. Beside him, as a representative of the more familiar seeking, suffering, or—as in the goldsmith Leonhard—ruling humanity of opera, the baritone as Doktor Faust seems an almost derivative figure, a symbol of the insuperable limitations of man, the human being—as contrasted with the tenor, a tonal spirit. In the opposition of the two, the play unfolds: whether, as in DIE BRAUTWAHL, in such form that the tenor, suffering ludicrously from his strange character, strives to become a human being again; or in ironic parody, as in the Cavaliere Leandro of ARLECCHINO; or, finally, as in DOKTOR FAUST, where the tenor altogether consciously dominates his spiritual sphere from the very beginning. Here the battle between the tragedy of humanity (baritone) and the superiority of the spirit (tenor) becomes an acute confrontation of opposites, in which both receive final formulation.

Everything else in Busoni's work does service to the clarification and contrast of these two basic forces. But they are conceived from an altogether tonal standpoint. Their existence is possible only through this creative view of the nature and effect of the singing voice. The fact that Busoni knew how to give form to this great and infinitely productive subject only by making most conscious use of the artificial device of historical opera, is similar in significance to the fact that the creators of opera themselves imitated ancient forms. The urge to musical creation, the singing germ of a new idea of opera, comes into existence before the mould that gives it form. Thus Busoni takes refuge in a historical model, which he adapts as well as possible to his basic purpose: to permit the form that lies hidden in the singing voice to unfold.

Busoni's dramatic idea is old: contrast between man and spirit in FAUST, between earthly disguise and an ironic view of true nature in BRAUTWAHL and ARLECCHINO. In principle these are all the same dramatic opposites. Linguistically and musically they are viewed through the same temperament, formed by the same hand, varied only in their surroundings according to the need of the moment. The Italian (in fact, the Latin) virtuoso in the twin-being that was Busoni, knew how to sing and to act, and the German knew how to give precision to his thoughts and to create an intellectual and spiritual unity.

At this point a level is attained to maintain which is to court the danger of diminishing popularity for the opera. For the central significance of the love-story in 19th-century opera contributed to its exceptionally wide appeal and appropriateness to the purposes of entertainment. There was no prospect of far-reaching consequences for the way in which Busoni, at least, formulated his theme. For especially tricky problems were connected with this approach: in the new orchestral treatment, taking account of French analytical harmony; in the scenic construction which was analytically arranged, not dynamic; in the special, commentating use to which the chorus was put; and in the romantic irony of the whole, as illustrated by the decorative and magic technique of the stage action.

6

Such is the situation that confronted the younger generation when it began to express itself after the war. It had no complete acquaintance with Busoni's work. His earlier operas, especially DIE BRAUTWAHL, have been only infrequently given, and DOKTOR FAUST reached the boards only in 1925, after Busoni's death.

But there ensued a liberation of the spirit that carried forward new ideas as upon invisible waves. In addition, Strawinsky was gradually becoming known. He made a strong impression upon the younger generation—ever searching, ever inclined to experiment and small-scale art—by the complete sureness of his mastery of every material, by the formal clarity of his structure despite apparent boldness, by his almost somnambulistic precision. He wrote no operas, at least in the beginning—only great pantomimes. In them the orchestra, especially as regards rhythm, plays so large and so decisive a part that singing voices are swallowed up, or become superfluous; only mute gesture remains.

Strawinsky at first evaded to a certain extent the problem of the singing voice. The voice was too sensuously realistic for his tragic and ironic view of life. He raised it to inaudible greatness, or, as in L'HISTOIRE DU SOLDAT, he uses the speaking voice as an abbreviation for it. Thus in approaching the voice Strawinsky traveled the same road as Strauss. Song disentangles itself only gradually, in Strauss from the intellectually motivated orchestra, and in Strawinsky from dance gesture. In MAVRA it takes shape in a merry women's trio with tenor, and in ŒDIPUS in a strictly stylized solemn cantata wearing the mask of Handel. Strawinsky loves to use style as a mask; it is for him an essential means of variation. He shares with Busoni the creative

ude towards the theatre,
istic brevity. He is less
siderations than Busoni,
gesture, with unfailing

al phenomena, operas of
nposers cropped up. They
Hindemith in his one-act
UNG ÜBER DEN SCHATTEN
rks based on old models.
achieved in WOZZECK a
ough its volcanic intensity
ersed the direction of the
wth of Wagner's operas,
ions.
hing and the groping. It
the fact that in opera as
leologies but the meaning
and the worth of the substance that are decisive. Application of this realization is not simple, to be sure, for here conditioning circumstances of many sorts are combined. Most important of these circumstances is the fact that the singing voice is least approachable from the point of view of instrumental function. Everything can be demonstrated much more clearly and easily in instrumental music. And yet the lure of the theatre, with all its inexhaustible possibilities, its breadth of

effect, above all, the indestructible and eternally new beauty of its material, remains. That the voice is indeed the material that contains the key to the theatre becomes increasingly clear with deepening knowledge, and through the standstill of symphonic, instrumental opera.

The struggle has begun for the reconquest of the operatic stage, which in essence is the struggle to win back the key to the secrets of the voice.

The composers of the generation born about 1900, especially, attempt this task over and over again: Hindemith, Křenek, Milhaud, and Weill. Of all these, Křenek, child of the theatre, is closest to the older opera, at least as regards his tonal and dramatic schemes. After the revolutionary-socialist purpose of his first work, ZWINGBURG, Křenek returns to the love-plot—in SPRUNG ÜBER DEN SCHATTEN satiric and in ORPHEUS psychoanalytic in tendency. JONNY is ruled by a new will to life, breaking through all sentimental considerations with an elemental flow of animal spirits. With its vigorous nonchalance, and its incorporation of types drawn from actual life, JONNY was the first big operatic success of this generation. This was due to the cleverness with which it combines familiar operatic types, a vocal style inclined towards that of the operatic, and dance gesture characteristic of the time. The fact that the whole sprang from an ironic purpose was overlooked, as was the serious intent of the lyric parts.

Thus was formed the new concept of jazz opera, which, to say the least, did not come up to its intentions. Křenek's Leben des Orest is a work similar to Jonny, but less concentrated, and less well designed in accord with the action. The central baritone figure remains. It is given musical form and made to sing through the most varied types of external events; chorus and ballet are incorporated to a considerable extent. The variety of grand opera becomes an alluring phantom. It points the way to the formation of vocal ensembles out of the figures of a new and fantastic world which is seen as a whole, no longer dominated by the tension of the sexes.

In Hindemith's Cardillac, too, the baritone dominates—in this case as the embodiment of the creative urge, of the undissolved, indeed indissoluble, relation of giving and receiving between the artist and the world. Here is another non-erotic problem used to reveal new forms. These are related to the *concertante* style of opera before Gluck, with its purely objective consideration, apart from all sentiment. Hindemith also, like Křenek, employs all vocal means, especially choruses of oratorio-like breath. Everywhere the struggle goes forward against the opera of sentiment, of emotional conflict, against the opera in which woman's voice is prominent. Where the female voice is used, as in Neues vom Tage, it is used in mockery of its earnestness of expression. It sings coloratura passages, but the words make fun of the music. The derivative operatic quartet is a caricature of the feeling for ensemble, the dramatic direction of the couples is not towards union but towards separation. The sense of the choral ensemble as a grand summary of what has gone before is artificially exaggerated into its very opposite.

A still sharper mockery of the love opera follows in the DREIGROSCHENOPER of Brecht and Weill. In this work even the voice is deprived of its characteristic tonal impulses. It is confined to simple songs, couplets, intentionally stunted arias. There follows a contraction of phrases and forms similar to that of Strawinsky. But occasionally the seriously intended operatic scheme shines through and is recognizable as a parody of the genuine vocal urge to song. The impulse towards a new enlivening of the voice and new vocal effects is continually active. It appears quite as genuinely serious and deeply searching in the artistic parody of earlier conventions of song by Hindemith and Weill as in the attempt to set new creative goals by the erection of new significances for tone: in JONNY, OREST, Milhaud's CHRISTOPHE COLOMBE, and CARDILLAC. The school-opera, like WIR BAUEN EINE STADT, in fact the entire tendency towards artless community music lacking in all artistic pretension, is based upon the same urge.

The latest and most vigorous attempt in this direction

is Weill's Bürgschaft. Like Křenek's first work, Zwingburg, it is concerned with a folk-plot. The sound of the chorus determines the dramatic and tonal architecture. This work, too, is a men's opera—indeed an opera of men's voices in the lower registers. The light color of the tenor is confined to a few lyric and character episodes: the action is between the main figure of the baritone and the companion figure of the bass. This fact alone accounts for the sombre coloring of the work. Similarly, the simple *lied*-like melodic idiom arises from the sound of the chorus and the simple coloring of the solo voices. It does not exclude passionate emotions, especially for the baritone, but it stamps them with a new stylization, clear, rooted in popular emotions, and purged of all pathos.

A different type of connection between speech and song is here evident. It was recognizable already in the Dreigroschenoper and Mahagonny and further developed in Silbersee. It rests not upon a welding of the two elements and their mutual intensification, but upon the parallel courses of speech and song on different but closely related levels. The unity of the languages of words and melody is no longer organic; it is now a partnership—based upon the skeptical realization of the impossibility of really uniting the two elements except by the direct sound-welding of the love song.

Thus the voice loses its functional significance as the organ for the expression of man's sexual nature. Nor does it any longer represent a character type, in Verdi's sense. It is at the same time objectified and led back upon itself. That type of voice for which such objectification is hardest, because its connection with the sensuous is almost unbreakable—the female voice—loses more and more of its creative importance. It is confined to episodic illustration or else diverted into quasi-instrumental coloratura singing. In newer works it is almost entirely excluded as a part of the dramatic action.

The same is true of the tenor as lover. He disappears as such, and receives a new significance as a character figure of ironic spirituality. The baritone does not have this character. He is the last surviving figure of an earlier time. The objectification of the baritone is most difficult because human emotion is the essential element of the baritone's vocal quality. Thus the course of the action springs from the struggle of the baritone either to rise from his own world of passionate expression into a passionless tonal sphere, or else to subordinate that sphere. Here is the nub of the stylistic problem in vocal treatment, of the gradual leveling-off to a vocal style without sentiment or emotion. In proportion as these qualities are taken away from the voice, its truly natural tone, apart from the expression of emotion, comes to the fore again. Thus the road is reopened to the inner nature of the voice, and the theatrical concept loses the connotation of operatic play-acting in the bad sense.

For this vocal style, the song has so far shown itself to be the best available, though doubtless not the conclusive, form. Its realization demands the compression of all other factors, hitherto used as extended expressive means: orchestral harmony and coloring, scenic apparatus, choral writing. Just as hitherto it had been the *expansive,* so now it is the concise, *intensive,* means of expression that predominates: above all, rhythm, which as such achieves decisive influence upon the relation between speech and song; then melody, which must now aim at the most pregnant and intense simplicity, and which more and more dissolves its relation to the instrumental dance type of melody and approaches ever more closely the natural tones of song.

All voices that correspond to this basic requirement are preferred; all whose nature leads them in other directions are left in the background. The theme of the action and the nature of the artistic realization are based upon these prerequisites. They correspond to deeply flowing spiritual currents of a non-rational nature. At the same time they make clear the necessity for constant change in the creative approach to the nature of the voice.

7

The question suggests itself whether, even if the symptoms have been correctly identified, their significance has been rightly valued.

Are the voices really the decisive factors in the tonal organism? If their predominance in the early history of the opera is granted, is there not perhaps a later shift in the equilibrium, through the strengthening of other creative elements: harmony, orchestra, dramatic idea? The question is the more difficult to answer since the descent of the complete operatic organism from the voice has never been scientifically, theoretically, or aesthetically investigated. If the claim were true, would not some such investigation inevitably have been made?

The implied deduction would be inaccurate. This is not a lesson to composers or a matter of historical analysis. It is the formulation of a deeply rooted organic process. The observation upon which such a formulation is based is possible—in the face of such hesitation and lack of clarity as have been displayed in the failure of previous methods of observation—only after a series of metamorphoses covering a period of several centuries.

But is it really possible to attribute so great a significance to the voice, and thus to consider so many other factors as subordinate or secondary?

Opinions on the productive relations of the singing

voice to other elements may at first remain divided. But the fact remains that in the course of the opera's development over several centuries, the singing voice has been the only primary defining factor in the nature of the species, and has remained essentially unchanged throughout the process. Such changes as it has displayed, moreover, have always been typical of the cultural atmosphere in which they occurred, either reflecting the development in the work of a great master, or determining the basis of the works of an entire period. The fact remains, finally, that the series of individual cases forms a strong and cogent organic sequence.

These facts characterize the voice as the only natural force in the opera—capable of all possible variety while fundamentally unchanging—and thus as the real criterion of the species. Its surface variations reveal the life-process of the opera. From these variations the realization of the whole and the conditions governing its metamorphoses must be inferred.

For the art-work as a whole, the objective significance of the other factors—technical, organic, or spiritual in nature—is quite another matter. It is even possible, since the nature of creation and the stimuli that bring it about are subjective and various, that these factors in individual cases may have their influence upon the conception itself. No musician will first plan his vocal scheme and then seek a framework of action to fit it. The creator himself must believe that he is following other laws, and the listener may at first believe that they are other laws that he observes. Here it becomes a question not of discovering these laws, but of recognizing the basic biological categories of characterization—of the elements, that is, that the creative spirit uses in order to be able to arrive at some conception. If these are continually overlooked or disdained, there is danger that the conditions governing the life of the species will be increasingly misunderstood, and that the species itself may gradually die off for lack of new natural material.

Richly productive periods carry their basic law within them, and obey it unconsciously. But where this instinctive knowledge leaves off, artificial construction begins. The greater the restrictions, requiring exceptional strength to overcome them, the more this artificial construction is fraught with danger. In French and German opera, these restrictions continually arise out of the intractability of the singing voice, intensified as it is by the difficulty of connecting the respective languages with singing tone. The problem is further infinitely complicated in the singing of translated—that is to say, wholly inorganic—texts.

These natural difficulties, ever intensified by singing practice, explain the many attempts in German opera to achieve an operatic result through some means other than song—through the orchestra, or through some intellectual approach or other. For the evaluation of such attempts it makes little difference whether they are "idealistic" or parodistic in intent. They are the more readily understandable since as a result of the education and aesthetic preparation of the opera-composer hardly any other means of expression is so remote from him, so unfamiliar in its special characteristics, as the human voice. And how is he to approach it creatively, how give it form, if he does not know it at all, if he is a stranger to it, if it is for him only one instrument among many? If he is thus unable to listen to it creatively, and if the general attitude and the consensus of critical opinion also lacks this creative approach?

The opera-composer must be a singer again, the ideal singer of his music; he must conceive out of the experience and the constant inner consciousness of the living voice. The sound of this living voice must permeate his entire work and be its foundation—that is the inescapable prerequisite of living opera.

The new opera, despite these difficulties, manifests an inner direction precisely in its approach to the voice. The primal instinct of the species conquers even the blindness of its creators, and keeps to its course even under limitations that rob it of some of its force. At any rate, the work of present-day composers is not nearly sufficient to meet the demand. Thus the older operas in all languages have to be pressed into service for the use of today's public. This state of affairs, which militates against the creation of an opera which would be truly of its time, would have been unthinkable at the time of Mozart, and conceivable even for the first half of the 19th century only with considerable reservations. The various historically and psychologically conditioned vocal types—grown out of tangible actuality and thus ephemeral figures—are now displayed in a colorful series meeting only the need for continual change. The means of unifying them and making them applicable to the present day is the stage setting, which becomes the spectator's common denominator of present-day opera.

But the setting, according to its origin, is only a consequence and a supplementary phenomenon to the voice expressing itself in song. Thus the relation is inverted. Cause becomes effect and effect cause. The action and all the elements of the opera connected with it become the central factors—the song-play (*Sing-Spiel*) becomes a play for the eye (*Schau-Spiel*). Every critical standard, every standard of artistic validity, loses its application. These standards cannot apply since the basic principles of the species are stood on their heads. Thus false ideas of performance take their place beside false ideas of conception. The resultant confusion in connection with the scenic guise of even the old works helps to place obstacles in the way of the natural development of new works and the recognition of the laws governing the species.

And so, since men no longer know how to adjust themselves to opera, they invent the legend of its being obsolete.

Thus the chief obstacle to opera at present is not the lack of creative talents. It results above all from the false approach to older works, from a continual faulty emphasis in opera as produced, and from a misrepresentation of history in the false and unreal guise of the present. Genuine timeliness is possible only if one proceeds from the root of the opera: the singing voice. If it is properly heard, it embraces in its tone the entire work, including the stylistic character of the full score.

It is therefore a mistake to think that the scenic dramaturgy of the opera is governed by no laws, and that it must derive its laws from those of the drama. If this idea is followed through to its conclusion it will always encounter difficulties: in the scenic formation of individual characters, arias, monologues, even more in the ensembles and finales—in fact in every particular, from the least to the most important. The scenic dramaturgy of the opera, in contrast to that of the drama, is so thoroughly predetermined that it limits freedom of interpretation much more than does the spoken word. It is like a play for which the author has tailored the players' costumes, for that is the real sense of the process of vocal stylization and characterization.

Thus the opera is a picture for the ear, gradually growing visible. It reflects in the course of its development the most vivid images of man: his voice as the basic dimension and basic material of the most varied characterization, as an emotional gesture, as a picture of natural man, as a play of virtuosity, as the call of love, as a mark of character, as the play of love, as the means of intellectual illumination of both individual and collective problems. Always, however, and in every new metamorphosis, the formation of characters out of this vocal material is the point of departure for the creative act.

If one glances over the entire series of these metamorphoses, disregarding detail, a curious basic phenomenon is to be seen in the changing vocal relation of the sexes to each other. From the *castrato* opera to the end of the lyric opera, woman's voice in the greatest possible variety always either predominates, or, as in Mozart and Verdi, is an almost equal partner of the male voice. From this point on, the female voice as a predominant figure noticeably begins to retire. Parallel phenomena are the momentary extinction, or at least eclipse, of Latin production, the primarily experimental character of German opera, and the preference for men's voices in important new works. This observation points to a change which is basic for the nature of the species. Through the accurate recognition of symptoms and causes, it makes understandable the hesitant, problematic qualities of contemporary operá as resulting from a crisis of uncertainty especially in regard to the vocal guise in which the sexes are to be clothed and even to the treatment of the voice as such—in regard, in short, to what the voice stands for: man himself. For man *is* the voice, viewed from one particular aspect.

Man is eternal, but he assumes changing forms. To-day he is no longer the sensual creature of the emotions that he was in the 18th and 19th centuries. That man of nature, descended from Rousseau, animated by the impulse of the species, has run his course. He has made his exit, just as the urge towards nature caused the vocal ideal of an earlier time, the *castrato* voice, to disappear.

Meanwhile, he is neither a mechanistic being nor a primeval creature. His new form shows itself at first only in outlines. But that out of the confusion of the contemporary scene a spiritual being of a newly religious nature will arise, can be foreseen by the prophetic vision of art. Art will be the first to come in contact with him, for where art is genuine it always creates out of a vision of things to come.

In the ability to create such a being out of the voice, the creative power of the musician shows itself. If he asks for a "book," it is because he wants the material out of which to create his characters. They are brought to life only by the living breath that the musician breathes into them. This living breath is song—for what is song, essentially, but sounding breath? It is the process of creation, and its fruit. It exists only when and as it sings. Every creative force that belongs to the opera takes its origin, receives its direction, and finds its fulfilment in the sound of the singing human voice, which is man himself translated into the sphere of tone, and through tone becoming visible again in a new form, born of tone.

Bird's-eye View of the History of Opera

(The titles of those works which are mentioned in the text are signified by an asterisk [*]. Some titles have been added only for the reader's information, but this list does not pretend to be complete.)

NAME OF COMPOSER	WORKS
PERI	*Dafne*, 1594
1561—1633	*Euridice*, 1600
MONTEVERDI	*Orfeo*, 1607
1567—1643	*Arianna*, 1608
	Il Ritorno d'Ulisse in Patria, 1630
	Adone, 1639
	L'Incoronazione di Poppea, 1642
LULLY	*Alceste*, 1674
1632—1687	*Bellérophon*, 1679
	Armide et Renaud, 1686
SCARLATTI	*La Rosaura*, 1690
1659—1725	*Teodora*, 1693
	Tigrane, 1715
	Griselda, 1721 (115 operas in all)

NAME OF COMPOSER	WORKS
KEISER 1674—1739	*Basilius*, 1693 *Störtebecker* *Die Leipziger Messe* *Ulysses*, 1722
RAMEAU 1683—1764	*Hippolyte et Aricie*, 1733 *Castor et Pollux*, 1737 *Dardanus*, 1739
HANDEL 1685—1759	*Almira*, 1705 *Agrippina*, 1709 *Rinaldo*, 1710 *Giulio Cesare*, 1724 *Berenice*, 1737
HASSE 1699—1783	*Tigrane*, 1723 *Sesostrate*, 1726 *Cleofide*, 1731
DUNI 1709—1775	*Le Peintre amoureux de son modèle*, 1757 *La Fée Urgèle*, 1765 *Les Moissoneurs*, 1768
PERGOLESI 1710—1736	* *La Serva padrona*, 1733
ROUSSEAU 1712—1778	* *Le Devin du village*, 1752

BIRD'S-EYE VIEW OF OPERA

NAME OF COMPOSER	WORKS
GLUCK 1714—1787	* *Orfeo*, 1762 * *Alceste*, 1767 * *Iphigénie en Aulide*, 1772 * *Armide*, 1777 * *Iphigénie en Tauride*, 1779
PHILIDOR 1726—1795	*Ernelinde, Princesse de Norvège*, 1767
ANONYMOUS	* *Beggar's Opera*, 1728
HILLER 1728—1804	*Der Teufel ist los*, 1766 *Lottchen am Hofe*, 1767 *Die Jagd*, 1776
MONSIGNY 1729—1817	*Le Déserteur*, 1769
DITTERSDORF 1739—1799	* *Doktor und Apotheker*, 1786
PAISIELLO 1740—1816	* *Il Barbiere di Siviglia*, 1782
GRÉTRY 1742—1813	*Les Deux Avares*, 1770 *Richard Cœur-de-Lion*, 1784 *Guillaume Tell*, 1791
CIMAROSA 1749—1801	* *Il Matrimonio segreto*, 1792
SCHENK 1753—1836	* *Der Dorfbarbier*, 1796

NAME OF COMPOSER	WORKS
MOZART 1756—1791	* *König Thamos*, 1773
	* *Idomeneo*, 1781
	* *Die Entführung aus dem Serail*, 1781
	* *Die Hochzeit des Figaro*, 1786
	* *Don Giovanni*, 1787
	* *Così fan tutte*, 1790
	La Clemenza di Tito, 1791
	* *Die Zauberflöte*, 1791
CHERUBINI 1760—1842	* *Lodoïska*, 1791
	* *Médée*, 1797
	* *Les Deux Journées* (*The Watercarriers*), 1800
	* *Faniska*, 1806
MÉHUL 1763—1817	* *Joseph*, 1807
BEETHOVEN 1770—1827	* *Fidelio*, 1805
SPONTINI 1774—1851	* *La Vestale*, 1807
	* *Fernand Cortez*, 1809
	* *Olympie*, 1819
ISOUARD 1775—1818	*Cendrillon*, 1810
BOÏELDIEU 1775—1834	* *La Dame blanche*, 1825

NAME OF COMPOSER	WORKS
HOFFMANN 1776—1822	*Undine*, 1814
AUBER 1782—1871	* *La Muette de Portici*, 1828 * *Fra Diavolo*, 1830
SPOHR 1784—1859	* *Faust*, 1816 * *Jessonda*, 1823
WEBER 1786—1826	* *Freischütz*, 1821 * *Euryanthe*, 1823 * *Oberon*, 1825
MEYERBEER 1791—1864	* *Robert le Diable*, 1831 * *Les Huguenots*, 1836 * *Le Prophète*, 1848 * *L'Africaine*, 1865 (Performed)
ROSSINI 1792—1868	* *Il Barbiere di Siviglia*, 1816 * *Guillaume Tell*, 1829
MARSCHNER 1795—1861	* *Der Vampyr*, 1828 * *Der Templer und die Jüdin*, 1829 * *Hans Heiling*, 1833
MERCADANTE 1795—1870	*Il Giuramento*, 1837
DONIZETTI 1797—1848	*Lucia di Lammermoor*, 1835 *La Fille du régiment*, 1840 *Linda di Chamounix*, 1842 * *Don Pasquale*, 1843

NAME OF COMPOSER	WORKS
HALÉVY 1799—1862	**La Juive*, 1835
BELLINI 1801—1835	**I Capuletti ed i Montecchi*, 1830 **Norma*, 1831 *I Puritani*, 1835
LORTZING 1801—1851	**Die beiden Schützen*, 1835 **Zar und Zimmermann*, 1837 **Hans Sachs*, 1840 **Der Wildschütz*, 1842 **Undine*, 1845 **Der Waffenschmied*, 1846 **Regina*, 1848
BERLIOZ 1803—1869	**Benvenuto Cellini*, 1838 **Roméo et Juliette*, 1839 **La Damnation de Faust*, 1846 *Les Troyens*, 1859 *Béatrice et Bénédict*, 1862
ADAM 1803—1856	**Le Postillon de Lonjumeau*, 1836
NICOLAI 1810—1849	**Die lustigen Weiber von Windsor* (*The Merry Wives of Windsor*), 1849
THOMAS 1811—1896	**Mignon*, 1866 *Hamlet*, 1868

BIRD'S-EYE VIEW OF OPERA

NAME OF COMPOSER	WORKS
WAGNER	* *Die Feen*, 1833
1813—1883	* *Das Liebesverbot*, 1836
	* *Rienzi*, 1842
	* *Der fliegende Holländer*, 1843
	* *Tannhäuser*, 1845
	* *Lohengrin*, 1847
	* *Das Rheingold*, 1854
	* *Die Walküre*, 1856
	* *Tristan und Isolde*, 1859
	* *Die Meistersinger*, 1867
	* *Siegfried*, 1869
	* *Die Götterdämmerung*, 1874
	* *Parsifal*, 1882
VERDI	* *Nabucco*, 1842
1813—1901	* *Ernani*, 1844
	* *Rigoletto*, 1851
	* *Il Trovatore*, 1853
	* *La Traviata*, 1853
	* *I Vespri siciliani*, 1855
	* *Un Ballo in maschera*, 1858
	* *Don Carlos*, 1867
	* *Aïda*, 1871
	* *Otello*, 1887
	* *Falstaff*, 1892 (26 operas in all)
GOUNOD	* *Faust*, 1859
1818—1893	* *Roméo et Juliette*, 1867

NAME OF COMPOSER	WORKS
OFFENBACH 1819—1880	* *Orphée aux enfers*, 1858 * *La Belle Hélène*, 1864 * *Les Contes d'Hoffmann*, 1881 (performed)
CORNELIUS 1824—1874	* *Der Barbier von Bagdad*, 1858 *Der Cid*, 1865
SMETANA 1824—1884	* *The Bartered Bride*, 1866 *Dalibor*, 1868 *The Kiss*, 1876 *Libussa*, 1881
SAINT-SAËNS 1835—1921	* *Samson et Dalila*, 1877
BIZET 1838—1875	*Les Pècheurs de perles*, 1863 *Djamileh*, 1872 * *Carmen*, 1875
MOUSSORGSKY 1839—1881	* *Boris Godunoff*, 1874 *Khovantchina*, 1886 (performed)
GÖTZ 1840—1876	* *Der Widerspänstigen Zähmung* (*The Taming of the Shrew*), 1874
TSCHAIKOVSKY 1840—1893	*Eugene Onegin*, 1878 *Pique-dame*, 1890
DVOŘÁK 1841—1904	*Russalka*, 1901 *Armida*, 1904

BIRD'S-EYE VIEW OF OPERA

NAME OF COMPOSER	WORKS
Massenet 1842—1912	* *Manon* * *Werther*, 1886
Humperdinck 1854—1921	* *Hänsel und Gretel*, 1893 *Königskinder*, 1908 *Die Heirat wider Willen*, 1905
Janaček 1854—1928	*Jenufa*, 1902 *Makropolus*, 1926 *Totenhaus*, 1928
Puccini 1858—1924	* *Willis*, 1884 * *Manon Lescaut*, 1893 * *Bohème*, 1896 * *Tosca*, 1900 * *Madama Butterfly*, 1904 *La Fanciulla del West*, 1910 * *Gianni Schicchi*, 1918 * *Turandot*, 1926 (performed)
Leoncavallo 1858—1919	* *I Pagliacci*, 1892
Charpentier 1860	* *Louise*, 1900
Wolf 1860—1903	* *Der Corregidor*, 1895
Debussy 1862—1918	* *Pelléas et Mélisande*, 1902

NAME OF COMPOSER	WORKS
MASCAGNI 1863	* *Cavalleria Rusticana*, 1890 *Nerone*, 1934
D'ALBERT 1864—1929	* *Die Abreise*, 1898 * *Kain*, 1900 * *Tiefland*, 1903 * *Die toten Augen*, 1916
STRAUSS 1864	* *Guntram*, 1894 * *Feuersnot*, 1901 * *Salome*, 1906 * *Elektra*, 1908 * *Rosenkavalier*, 1910 * *Ariadne auf Naxos*, 1912 * *Die Frau ohne Schatten*, 1919 * *Intermezzo*, 1924 * *Die Ægyptische Helena*, 1928 *Arabella*, 1933 *Die schweigsame Frau*, 1935
DUKAS 1865—1935	* *Ariane et Barbe-bleue*, 1907
BUSONI 1866—1924	* *Die Brautwahl*, 1912 * *Turandot*, 1918 * *Arlecchino*, 1918 * *Doktor Faust*, 1925 (performed)
GIORDANO 1867	*Andrea Chénier*, 1896 *Madame Sans-Gêne*, 1915

NAME OF COMPOSER	WORKS
PFITZNER 1869	**Der Arme Heinrich*, 1893 **Die Rose vom Liebesgarten*, 1900 **Palestrina*, 1915 **Das Herz*, 1932
SCHÖNBERG 1874	**Erwartung* **Die glückliche Hand*, 1927 (performed) **Von heute bis morgen*, 1930
RAVEL 1875	*L'Heure espagnole*, 1907
WOLF-FERRARI 1876	*Le Donne curiose*, 1903 *I Gioielli Della Madonna*, 1908 *Il Segreto di Susanna*, 1909 *Sly*, 1927
ALFANO 1877	*La Resurrezione*, 1904 *Sakuntala*, 1921 *Madonna ymperia*, 1927
SCHREKER 1878—1934	**Der ferne Klang*, 1909 *Die Prinzessin und das Spielwerk*, 1911 **Die Gezeichneten*, 1918 **Der Schatzgräber*, 1920 *Irrelohe*, 1924 *Der singende Teufel*, 1929 *Der Schmied von Gent*, 1932

NAME OF COMPOSER	WORKS
PEDROLLO 1878	*Raskolnikoff*, 1926
STRAWINSKY 1882	* *Pétrouchka*, 1912 * *L'Histoire du soldat*, 1918 * *Mavra*, 1922 * *Œdipus*, 1927 *Perséphone*, 1934
MALIPIERO 1882	*L'Orfeide*, 1920 *Filomela*, 1928
CASELLA 1883	*Donna serpenta*, 1933
GRUENBERG 1883	*Emperor Jones*, 1933
TAYLOR 1885	*Peter Ibbetson*, 1930
BERG 1885	* *Wozzeck*, 1926 *Lulu*, 1935 (not performed)
MILHAUD 1892	* *Christophe Colombe*, 1926 *Le Pauvre Matelot*, 1927 *Minute-operas*, 1928 *Juarez et Maximilian*, 1929
HINDEMITH 1895	*Three one-act operas*, 1921 * *Cardillac*, 1926 * *Neues vom Tage*, 1929

NAME OF COMPOSER	WORKS
	Mathis der Maler, 1935 (not performed)
CASTELNUOVO-TEDESCO 1895	*Mandragola*, 1923
WEINBERGER 1896	*Schwanda*, 1927
KŘENEK 1900	* *Die Zwingburg*, 1922 * *Der Sprung über den Schatten*, 1923 * *Orpheus*, 1923 * *Jonny*, 1927 *Three one-act operas*, 1928 * *Orest*, 1929 *Das Leben Karls V*, 1934 (not performed)
WEILL 1900	* *Mahagonny*, 1927 * *Dreigroschenoper*, 1928 * *Der Jasager*, 1930 * *Die Bürgschaft*, 1931 * *Der Silbersee*, 1932

INDEX

Index